Student Solutions Mai

for

Wood, Wood, and Boyd

Mastering the World of Psychology

Second Edition

prepared by

David Wasieleski
Valdosta State University

PEARSON

Boston   New York   San Francisco
Mexico City   Montreal   Toronto   London   Madrid   Munich   Paris
Hong Kong   Singapore   Tokyo   Cape Town   Sydney

ISBN 0-205-47807-7

Printed in the United States of America

10 9 8 7 6 5 4 3   09 08 07 06 05

Table of Contents

Student Practice Tests Solutions

Chapter 1 - Practice Test 1

1.   Psychology is defined as:

Answer: (C) the scientific study of behavior and mental processes. Page: 3

2.   A counseling psychologist is working with a married couple to promote better communication in their relationship. Which goal of psychology is the psychologist trying to accomplish?

Answer: (D) influence   Page: 4

3.   Unlike basic research, applied research is intended to:

Answer: (A) solve practical problems.   Page: 5

4.   The first psychological laboratory was established by:

Answer: (C) Wilhelm Wundt.   Page: 5

5.   The early school of psychology devoted to studying the basic elements of conscious mental experiences was:

Answer: (B) structuralism.   Page: 6

6.   What problem was common to early female researchers in the field of psychology?

Answer: (C) The schools they attended refused to confer advanced degrees.   Page: 7

7.   Which figure is most associated with the school of behaviorism, which studies only observable, measurable behavior?

Answer: (A) John B. Watson   Page: 8

8.   Dr. Smith believes that depression is a consequence of faulty thinking. With which theoretical perspective would Dr. Smith most agree?

Answer: (D) cognitive   Pages: 9-10

9.   A researcher is studying patterns of social play in 8-year-olds by watching children on a playground and documenting their behaviors. She is using which research method?

Answer: (D) naturalistic observation   Page: 11

10.   A survey-taker makes sure that the people surveyed closely mirror the population of interest. He is making sure that he has a:

Answer: (A) representative sample.   Page: 12

11.   A professor asks her class to record how often they study. Her students may tend to report studying more than they really do, thereby giving:

Answer: (B) a social desirability response.   Page: 13

12.   The variable that is presumed to vary as a result of the manipulation of another variable is called:

Answer: (B) a dependent variable.   Page: 15

13.   Dr. Needles is testing the effects of a new drug. One group receives the drug, while a comparison group receives an injection of a harmless solution. The group that receives the drug is called the:

Answer: (A) experimental group.   Page: 15

14.   In Dr. Needles' experiment, neither he nor the participants know who gets the drug and who gets the harmless solution. This method is called:

Answer: (B) the double-blind method.   Page: 16

15.   Which of the following correlation coefficients indicates the strongest relationship between two variables?

Answer: (C) -0.85   Page: 17

16.   Research participants must be told the purpose of the study in which they are participating, and its potential for harming them. This is the ethical consideration known as:

Answer: (D) informed consent.   Page: 19

17.   Which of the following is *not* a characteristic exhibited when one engages in critical thinking?

Answer: (C) open-minded acceptance   Page: 21

18.   Dr. Jarrod, a psychologist, is part of an interdisciplinary team with biologists, biochemists, and medical researchers, who study the nervous system. To which field does Dr. Jarrod likely belong?

Answer: (D) neuroscience   Page: 24

19.   Dr. Benson is studies the factors that promote productivity in an office environment for a large company. Which type of psychologist is Dr. Benson likely to be?

Answer: (B) industrial-organizational psychologist   Page: 26

20.   Which type of psychologist is most likely to study how human behavior is affected by the presence of other people?

Answer: (A) social psychologist   Page: 26

21.   Replication is used to verify that a study's findings are accurate with a different group of participants.

Answer: True   Page: 4

22.   Wilhelm Wundt and William James belonged to the same early school of psychology.

Answer: False   Page: 6

23.   Humanistic psychology focuses on the uniqueness of human beings and their capacity for growth.

Answer: True   Page: 9

24.   Descriptive research methods equally accomplish all three goals of psychology.

Answer: False   Page: 11

25.   Experiments allow for the greatest experimenter control as well as permitting cause and effect conclusions to be drawn.

Answer: True   Page: 13

26.   A perfect positive correlation is indicated by the coefficient 1.00.

Answer: True   Page: 17

27.   If stress and illness are positively correlated, that means that stress causes illness.

Answer: False   Page: 18

28.   APA permits the use of animals in research.

Answer: True   Page: 19

29.   Information-processing theory compares the human brain's workings to those of a computer.

Answer: True   Page: 10

30.   The view that human behavior is shaped by physiological factors is called the sociocultural approach.

Answer: False   Page: 24

31.   Explain what separates the science of psychology from common sense. Include in your response why a theory cannot rely on anecdotal evidence.

Answer: Common sense propositions are made based on experience or folklore. Common sense sayings may also contradict. For example, do "opposites attract" or do "birds of a feather flock together"? Psychology, as a science, employs the scientific method to investigate propositions through the use of research. The scientific method consists of the orderly, systematic process that researchers follow as they identify a research problem, design a study to investigate the problem, collect and analyze data, draw conclusions, and then communicate their findings.   Pages: 4-5, 21

32.   Name and describe four major psychological perspectives. According to each perspective selected, what is the primary reason for your behavior?

Answer: Psychologists seek to explain behavior and may do so in a number of different ways. Psychologists who take a biological perspective look to the functioning of the nervous system and the structure of the brain to explain human behavior. Psychologists who take a cognitive perspective focus on thinking as a means of explaining behavior, that how one thinks influences how one acts. Humanistic psychologists look at our desire to be the best that we can be as the guiding force behind our behavior, while the Freudian approach sees most of our behavior as the product of the unconscious.   Pages: 8-10

33.   Suppose you wanted to test whether a new drug helped improve scores on a memory test for college students. Design an experiment to do so. Include how you would select your sample, and label the independent and dependent variables, as well as the experimental and control groups. Also describe one confounding variable you would avoid.

Answer: Volunteers from one or more college campuses should be randomly assigned to the experimental group, the group that will receive the drug, and a control group, who will not receive the drug. This random assignment ensures that the two groups are roughly equivalent in all respects other than the receipt of the drug or a placebo. The use of a single-blind or double-blind design may prevent biases on the part of the participants or the researcher from impacting the results. All participants will then take a test of memory. The drug is the independent variable, and scores on the memory test are the dependent variable. If the drug is effective, the experimental group will outperform the control group on the test of memory.
Pages: 13-15

1. What separates psychology from simple common sense?

Answer: (C) reliance on the scientific method   Pages: 3-4

2.   Which term refers to a set of principles proposed to explain how a number of separate facts are related?

Answer: (A) theory   Page: 4

3.   Dr. Carson conducts an experiment and achieves results that support her theory. She conducts another study, hoping to achieve the same results as in the first experiment. What process is Dr. Carson conducting?

Answer: (B) replication   Page: 4

4.   Laura wants to find out why her boy friend has been so grumpy lately. Which goal of psychology is Laura trying to accomplish?

Answer: (B) explanation   Page: 4

5.   WilhelmWundt studied the perception of various sensory stimuli using the method of:

Answer: (C) introspection.   Page: 5

6.   The leading advocate of the early school of psychology devoted to the study of how humans use mental processes to adapt to their environment was:

Answer: (D) William James.   Page: 6

7.   Which school of psychology posits that individuals perceive objects and patterns as whole units?

Answer: (B) gestalt psychology   Page: 10

8.   The school of psychology led by Rogers and Maslow that emphasizes individual uniqueness and the capacity for growth is called:

Answer: (D) humanism.   Page: 9

9.   When a television network predicts the winner of an election, they are relying on which research method?

Answer: (A) a survey   Page: 12

10.   The factor that is manipulated by the researcher in an effort to determine its effects on something else is called:

Answer: (C) an independent variable.   Page: 14

11.   The group that does *not* receive exposure to the independent variable in an experiment is the:

Answer: (B) control group.   Page: 15

12.   Dr. Janus teaches two sections of Introductory Psychology, one at 8 am and one at 1 pm. He decides to conduct an experiment on the effect of using PowerPoint slides to lecture on the grades of each class. Students in the 1 pm section see PowerPoint slides for a lecture, whereas the students in the 8 am class see notes on a chalkboard. Dr. Janus plans to compare the performance on the exams, but a colleague points out that his study has a confounding variable. What is that confounding variable?

Answer: (D) the times of the two sections   Page: 15

13.   Which is an advantage of the experimental method?

Answer: (C) the ability to draw cause and effect conclusions   Page: 16

14.   "There is a positive correlation between ice cream sales and domestic violence reports." This statement suggests that:

Answer: (C) domestic violence calls increase and ice cream sales increase at the   same time.   Pages: 17-18

15.   Which of the following is a primary cause of participant-related bias?

Answer: (A) lack of representativeness in the sample   Page: 19

16.   Which of the following is *not* a provision of the APA's ethics code?

Answer: (B) Deception of subjects is always unethical.   Page: 19

17.   A theory has heuristic value when:

Answer: (A) it stimulates debate and motivates individuals to pursue research.   Page: 21

18.   A therapist utilizes techniques from a variety of theoretical approaches. Her approach would be said to be:

Answer: (B) eclectic.   Page: 25

19.   Adaptation and survival are central themes in the _____ school of psychology.

Answer: (C) evolutionary   Page: 22

20.   Dr. Runge diagnoses and treats individuals with severe mental disorders such as schizophrenia. Dr. Runge is most likely which type of psychologist?

Answer: (C) clinical psychologist   Page: 26

21.   The scientific method involves a systematic investigation that always leads to a solution of a real-world problem.

Answer: False   Page: 4

22.   Minority psychologists have grown in their representation in the field of psychology over the past several decades.

Answer: True   Page: 7

23.   The conscious mind is the primary focus of psychoanalysis.

Answer: False   Page: 9

24.   An experiment accomplishes both the goals of description and explanation.

Answer: True   Page: 13

25.   A research result is considered valid if the experiment contains confounding variables.

Answer: False   Page: 15

26.   A positive correlation between two variables means that the first variable causes the second; a negative correlation means the opposite.

Answer: False   Pages: 17-18

27.   Debriefing is required as soon as possible after a study if deception has been used.

Answer: True   Page: 19

28. One reason for using animals in research is that more medical procedures can be done on animals than on humans.

Answer: True   Page: 20

29. The different perspectives in psychology differ only in how they explain abnormal behavior.

Answer: False   Page: 22

30. Developmental psychologists specialize in doing therapy with children.

Answer: False   Page: 26

31. Describe the four basic goals of psychology, and come up with a real-world example of each.
Answer: Description, explanation, prediction, and control are the four basic goals of psychology. Psychologists can use observational research methods to collect information to describe behavior. Experiments can be conducted to seek explanations for why things happen. A variety of research methods may be used to better predict the conditions under which a behavior occurs, as when correlational data are used to determine the relationship between variables. Psychologists also strive to determine what controls behavior, so that efforts can be made to encourage desirable actions and discourage undesirable actions.   Pages: 4-5

32. Describe the differences between an experiment and the descriptive research methods. What are the advantages and disadvantages of each?

Answer: Experiments can be conducted when the researcher can control the variables of interest, allowing cause-and-effect relationships to be explored. Some research questions may not lend themselves to such approaches and must be explored by measuring existing variables. In a descriptive research study, variables are not manipulated, although they may be measured objectively or simply described. Descriptive research methods may allow conclusions to be made about the relationship between two variables, but cause-effect conclusions are not possible. Descriptive methods may also provide information about real-world phenomena, although such information may not be generalizable to other people or situations.   Pages: 11-13, 16-17

33.   Name and describe four types of psychologists, including what they do and the types of places in which they work.

Answer: Clinical psychologists specialize in the diagnosis and treatment of mental and behavioral disorders. Most work in clinics, hospitals, or private practices, and many work at colleges and universities. Counseling psychologists help people with less severe problems, and may provide academic or vocational counseling. Most work in a school or university, and some may have a private practice. Experimental psychologists specialize in conducting research in virtually any area of psychology, and usually work in a laboratory setting, often in colleges or universities. Developmental psychologists are experimental psychologists who conduct research on how people grow, develop, and change over the life span. Educational psychologists study teaching and learning, and may help to train teachers. Most work in school or college settings. Social psychologists are experimental psychologists who specialize in studying how people behave around others. Industrial/organizational psychologists study the relationships between people and their work environments.   Page: 26

1.   The neurons that relay messages from the sense organs to the central nervous system are:

Answer: (A) afferent (sensory) neurons.   Page: 37

2.   Which part of the neuron receives messages from other cells?

Answer: (A) dendrite   Page: 38

3.   When a neuron's axon carries a positive electrical potential of about 50 millivolts, it is said to be firing. This is called the:

Answer: (C) action potential.   Page: 38

4.   Sarah seems to be depressed. In addition, she isn't sleeping well and has little appetite. Which neurotransmitter is most likely to be involved in the problem?

Answer: (A) serotonin   Page: 41

5.   Jesse is wiring together his home theater system, and he accidentally touches a live wire, getting a painful shock and quickly jerks his hand away. The reflex of pulling his hand back is dictated by the:

Answer: (B) spinal cord.   Page: 43

6.   A severe injury to the medulla would likely result in:

Answer: (D) death.   Page: 43

7.   Which area of the brain regulates several body functions, including hunger, thirst, sexual behavior, and internal body temperature?

Answer: (B) the hypothalamus.   Page: 45

8.   Danielle is left-handed. When she is taking notes in class, which part of her brain is directing the movements of her hand?

Answer: (B) right frontal lobe   Page: 47

9.   The visual cortex is located in the:

Answer: (D) occipital lobe.   Page: 50

10.   Coral suffers from epilepsy. Her doctor wants to perform an operation that he believes will improve the quality of Coral's life. What is the most likely change that Coral's doctor wants to make in her brain?

Answer: (C) He plans to sever her corpus callosum.   Page: 52

11.   Which part of the nervous system is primarily tasked with regulating the body's internal environment?

Answer: (A) autonomic nervous system   Page: 58

12.   During an exam, which brain-wave pattern are you most likely to exhibit?

Answer: (B) beta wave   Page: 55

13.   Kelvin is having some tests run to look for signs of physical damage to his brain. He also needs to be sure that certain parts of his brain are actually working properly. Which type of diagnostic technique would reveal both structures and activity?

Answer: (A) fMRI   Page: 55

14.   Which individual is most likely to recover a lost brain function following a head injury?

Answer: (D) a 15-year-old girl   Pages: 56-57

15.   Which of the following statements about gender differences in the adult brain is *true*?

Answer: (D) Women have more gray matter in the area of the brain that controls emotions than do men.   Page: 57

16.   Marisa is riding a roller coaster. As it surges over the high point to plunge downward, her heart races, breathing quickens, and blood flow to her skeletal muscles increases. Which division of the peripheral nervous system is most active?

Answer: (C) sympathetic   Pages: 58-59

17.   Chemical substances that are released in one part of the body but affect other parts of the body are called:

Answer: (C) hormones.   Page: 59

18.   Which organ is responsible for regulating blood sugar by releasing insulin and glucagon into the blood stream?

Answer: (A) the pancreas   Page: 61

19.   In a dominant-recessive pattern set of inheritance rules, which pair of genes would result in the expression of a recessive trait?

Answer: (C) two recessive genes   Page: 62

20.   Which type of study is *not* likely to be used in the field of behavioral genetics?

Answer: (A) an experiment   Page: 63

21.   The myelin sheath allows neural impulses to travel faster.

Answer: True   Page: 39

22.   Any neurotransmitter can fit into any receptor.

Answer: False   Page: 40

23.   The limbic system is a series of brain structures involved in emotion.

Answer: True   Page: 45

24.   Wernicke's aphasia involves the difficulty with comprehension of speech.

Answer: True   Page: 50

25.   The right hemisphere is responsible for most language functions.

Answer: False   Page: 51

26.   Pain perception occurs in the somatosensory area of the cerebrum.

Answer: True   Page: 49

27.   The somatic nervous system can be divided into the sympathetic and parasympathetic nervous systems.

Answer: False   Page: 58

28.   An MRI scan is a more powerful way to view the brain than an EEG.

Answer: True   Page: 55

29.   The gonads are responsible for production of sex hormones.

Answer: True   Page: 61

30.   There are 22 pairs of chromosomes in the human body.

Answer: False   Page: 62

31.   Describe the process of neural conduction across the synapse.

Answer: The action potential is transmitted down the length of the axon, and reaches the axon terminal. Inside the axon terminal are small containers called synaptic vesicles, which hold chemicals called neurotransmitters. These neurotransmitters are released into the synaptic cleft. They have a distinctive molecular shape, which fit into specific receptor sites on the surfaces of cell bodies and dendrites. Once the neurotransmitter binds to a receptor site, it may have an excitatory (influencing the neuron to fire) or inhibitory (influencing the neuron not to fire) effect on the receiving neuron.   Pages: 38-40

32.   Name and describe the effects of five neurotransmitters.

Answer: Acetylcholine exerts excitatory effects on skeletal muscle fibers, influencing them to contract so the body can move. It also has an inhibitory effect on muscle fibers in the heart, so that the heart does not beat too rapidly. Acetylcholine also has an excitatory effect in stimulating neurons involved in learning new information and storing information in memory. Dopamine is related to functions such as learning, attention, movement, and reinforcement. Neurons in the brains of people with Parkinson's disease and schizophrenia appear to be less sensitive to the effects of dopamine. Norepinephrine affects eating, alertness, and sleep. Epinephrine affects the metabolism of glucose and nutrient energy stored in muscles to be released during strenuous exercise. Serotonin plays an important role in regulating mood, sleep, impulsivity, aggression, and appetite. Glutamate is the primary excitatory neurotransmitter in the brain, and is active in areas of the brain involved in learning, thought, and emotions. GABA is the main inhibitory neurotransmitter in the brain, and facilitates the control of anxiety in humans. Finally, endorphins are a class of neurotransmitters that reduce pain and the stress of vigorous exercise, and positively affect mood.   Pages: 41-42

33.   Review the specialized functions of the right and left hemispheres of the cerebral cortex.

Answer: The left hemisphere controls the right side of the body, and is responsible for most language functions, including speaking, writing, reading, speech comprehension, and comprehension of written information. The left hemisphere is also specialized for mathematics and logic as well as one's sense of well-being. The right hemisphere controls the left side of the body, and processes visual-spatial relations. Music processing, emotional thinking, and interpretation of nonverbal behavior also are specialties of the right hemisphere.   Pages: 51-52

1.   The neurons that carry signals from the central nervous system to organs, glands, and skeletal muscles are:

Answer: (B) efferent (motor) neurons.   Page: 37

2.   The gap between the axon terminal of one neuron and the dendrite of another neuron is the:

Answer: (D) synapse.   Page: 38

3.   The period of time (of about 1-2 seconds) during which it is impossible for a neuron to fire is called:

Answer: (B) the refractory period.   Page: 38

4.   Individuals with Alzheimer's disease often have difficulty learning new information and retaining it in memory. Which neurotransmitter is likely involved in this difficulty?

Answer: (D) acetylcholine   Page: 41

5.   The central nervous system is made up of:

Answer: (B) the brain and spinal cord.   Page: 42

6.   Which area of the brain is most crucial in your efforts to store information in long-term memory?

Answer: (D) the hippocampus   Page: 45

7.   Before traveling to higher brain centers, most sensory information must pass through the:

Answer: (B) thalamus.   Page: 45

8.   The auditory cortex is located in the:

Answer: (C) temporal lobe.   Page: 50

9.   Which part of the brain controls the pituitary gland?

Answer: (D) the hypothalamus   Page: 60

10.   John suffers a traumatic brain injury that makes it difficult for him to comprehend speech. The likely site of his injury is the:

Answer: (C) left temporal lobe.   Page: 50

11.   If the frontal lobe controls voluntary movements, then which division of the peripheral nervous system does the frontal lobe control?

Answer: (A) somatic   Page: 58

12.   Slice-by-slice cross sectional images of the brain are produced by the:

Answer: (C) CT scan.   Page: 55

13.   Which of the following is a specialized function of the left hemisphere of the brain in most people?

Answer: (A) control of the production of written language   Page: 51

14.   While in a deep sleep, which brain-wave pattern are you most likely to exhibit?

Answer: (C) delta wave   Page: 55

15.   Lenora is driving in heavy traffic and is suddenly "cut off" by a darting sedan. She is startled, but soon recovers her composure. Her heart rate and breathing slow to normal rates. Which division of the nervous system has taken over as she has calmed down?

Answer: (B) parasympathetic   Page: 59

16.   Jennifer was in an accident that caused some damage to her motor cortex. If she is able to walk again, it will be because of the _____ of parts of the brain.

Answer: (A) plasticity   Page: 48

17.   Which of the following is the most common cause of damage to adult brains?

Answer: (D) strokes   Page: 58

18.   Melatonin, the hormone that regulates sleep and wakefulness, is produced and regulated by the:

Answer: (B) pineal gland.   Page: 60

19.   In which of the following patterns of inheritance is a trait influenced by both genes and environmental factors?

Answer: (C) multifactorial inheritance   Page: 62

20.   Which of the following studies allows researchers to disentangle the effects of heredity and the environment?

Answer: (C) an adoption study   Page: 63

21.   The resting potential for a neuron is 50 millivolts.

Answer: False   Page: 38

22.   Dopamine is a neurotransmitter that is related to both schizophrenia and Parkinson's disease.

Answer: True   Page: 41

23.   Simple sobriety tests are designed to test the functioning of the cerebellum.

Answer: True   Page: 44

24.   The spinal cord is responsible for reflexes that help us avoid injury.

Answer: True   Page: 43

25.   The limbic system includes the hippocampus, the reticular formation, and the amygdala.

Answer: False   Page: 45

26.   The two cerebral hemispheres are connected by a band of nerves called the corpus callosum.

Answer: True   Page: 46

27.   As we age, the ability of the brain to reorganize itself and recover from damage is reduced.

Answer: True   Page: 57

28. If a split-brain patient is blindfolded, and is given a pen to hold in their left hand, she will not be able to name the object being held.

Answer: True   Page: 53

29. An EEG can reveal what is happening in individual neurons.

Answer: False   Page: 55

30. Fraternal twins result when two sperm cells fertilize a single egg.

Answer: False   Page: 63

31. Describe the various functions of the thalamus and hypothalamus.

Answer: The thalamus and hypothalamus both lie above the brain stem. The thalamus serves as the relay station for virtually all the information that flows into and out of the forebrain, including sensory information for all senses except smell. The thalamus also plays a small role in our ability to learn new verbal information and in producing language, as well as in helping to regulate the sleep cycle. The hypothalamus regulates hunger, thirst, sexual behavior, internal body temperature, and a variety of emotional behaviors. The hypothalamus also houses the biological clock, which is responsible for the timing of the sleep/wake cycle. Finally, the hypothalamus also directs the pituitary gland, and thus indirectly controls the endocrine system. Pages: 45

32. Name and describe the function of each of the four lobes of the brain.

Answer: The cerebral cortex can be divided into frontal, parietal, temporal, and occipital lobes. The frontal lobes are involved in planning and motor function. They contain Broca's area, a region involved in speech production, and also the motor cortex. The parietal lobes are involved in body senses and contain the somatosensory cortex. Wernicke's area is involved in speech comprehension and is found in the left temporal lobe. The temporal lobes are involved in audition. Finally, the occipital lobes are involved in vision and contain the primary motor cortex. Pages: 47-51

33.   Describe four glands and the hormones they produce, including the function of those hormones.

Answer: The pituitary gland releases hormones that activate other glands in the endocrine system, as well as the hormone responsible for body growth. The thyroid gland produces thyroxin, which regulates the rate at which food is metabolized, or transformed into energy. The adrenal glands produce hormones that prepare the body for emergencies and stressful situations, and also release corticoids and small amounts of the sex hormones. The pineal gland produces and regulates melatonin, which regulates sleep and wakefulness. The thymus gland produces hormones that are needed for the production of specialized white blood cells that destroy microorganisms that can cause diseases. Finally, the gonads produce sex hormones –androgens which influence sexual motivation, and estrogen and progesterone which regulate the menstrual cycle.   Pages: 59-61

Chapter 3 - Practice Test 1

1. Jenna accidentally steps on a pin. The stimulation of her skin and transmission of the information regarding this touch to the central nervous system is the process of:

Answer: (B) sensation.   Page: 74

2. In order to sense a change in weights being carried, the additional weight added must be 2% higher than what you carried before. This difference threshold is calculated using:

Answer: (A) Weber's law.   Page: 74

3. The process of converting sensory stimulation into neural impulses is called:

Answer: (D) transduction.   Page: 75

4. The outer part of the eye to which serves to protect the eye, and on which you would place your contact lenses, is called the:

Answer: (B) cornea.   Page: 76

5. On a rainy day, Jake sees that his flashy new red car doesn't look as bright and shiny. The color seems duller. This is because:

Answer: (A) Jake's rods are more relied upon, and rods don't allow color perception.   Page: 76

6. Connie squints to better see the board in class. She is trying to get the light waves to strike which part of her retina?

Answer: (C) the fovea   Page: 77

7. Which theory best explains visual phenomena like color vision and afterimages?

Answer: (B) Opponent-process theory   Page: 79

8. The loudness of a sound corresponds to which physical characteristic of a sound wave?

Answer: (A) amplitude   Page: 81

9. Which of the following is the sensory receptor for hearing?

Answer: (D) hair cells   Page: 82

10.   Which theory best explains how sensory receptors in our ear encode sound wave frequencies over 1000 Hz?

Answer: (B) place theory   Page: 83

11.   Glenda purchases some new perfume to attract her boy friend's attention. The perfume is meant to stimulate which sensory system?

Answer: (A) olfactory   Page: 83

12.   Linda's friends all drink coffee, but Linda finds the taste of coffee very bitter, more so than do her friends. What is one explanation for Linda's dislike of coffee?

Answer: (C) She is a "supertaster."   Page: 85

13.   Monique experiences a leg cramp in her calf. She massages the muscle while gritting her teeth and finds she feels less pain. What theory explains this decrease in pain?

Answer: (D) gate control theory   Page: 86

14.   A toddler plays with blocks by sorting them into piles by color, so that the red blocks make up one pile, the blue blocks a second pile, and the green blocks a third pile. She is using which Gestalt principle of perceptual organization?

Answer: (B) similarity   Page: 91

15.   Gary sees a friend standing near a fence. The fence partially blocks his view of his friend, so Gary realizes the fence is closer to him than is his friend. Which monocular depth cue is Gary using?

Answer: (C) interposition   Page: 93

16.   The "Old Woman/Young Woman" image is an example of:

Answer: (C) an ambiguous figure.   Page: 95

17.   Which of the following involves an illusion utilizing two equal lines with diagonals extending outward from one line, making it appear longer than the line with diagonals extending inward?

Answer: (A) the Müller-Lyer illusion   Page: 95

18.   Brandi is learning to read by sounding out a word one letter at a time. What type of processing is she using?

Answer: (A) bottom-up processing   Page: 90

19.   Leroy is studying and trying to ignore his roommate's phone conversation in the other room. He is engrossed in his psychology textbook until he hears his name mentioned, when he suddenly becomes aware of what his roommate is saying on the phone. What perceptual concept does this example demonstrate?

Answer: (D) the cocktail party phenomenon   Page: 88

20.   Which type of extra-sensory perception might be claimed by individuals who try to predict the outcome of a football game?

Answer: (C) precognition   Page: 97

21.   We perceive different colors based on the wavelength of light striking our retina.

Answer: True   Page: 75

22.   A blind spot exists in our vision because of an area on the retina with no visual receptors.

Answer: True   Page: 77

23.   Someone with color blindness cannot perceive any colors at all.

Answer: False   Page: 80

24.   The same note played on different instruments sound different because of timbre.

Answer: True   Page: 81

25.   The sensory receptors for the olfactory system are located in the olfactory bulbs.

Answer: False   Page: 84

26.   Different areas of the tongue specialize in processing different taste sensations.

Answer: False   Page: 84

27.   The body produces natural painkillers called endorphins.

Answer: True   Page: 86

28.   You are able to perceive a quarter as round even when viewing it on an angle due to perceptual constancy.

Answer: True   Page: 92

29.   Illusions fool our perceptual system only when our attention decreases.

Answer: False   Page: 95

30.   Subliminal perception can influence behavior to some degree.

Answer: True   Page: 97

31.   Explain the progression of a sound wave from its arrival at the eardrum to its arrival in the brain.

Answer: Sound waves are created by movement of the air. These waves strike the eardrum and the eardrum vibrates. The movement of the eardrum sets in motion the bones of the middle ear. The bones of the middle ear amplify the sound wave and then strike the oval window. On the other side of the oval window is the inner ear, a structure called the cochlea. When the oval window receives the sound wave, it sets the fluid contained in the cochlea into motion. In the cochlea are hair cells that bend as the fluid moves. When the hair cells bend, an electrical impulse is generated and it travels to the brain.   Page: 82

32.   Describe how gate-control theory explains both our perception of pain and how psychological factors affect this perception.

Answer: The gate-control theory of Mezack and Wall suggests that there is an area in the spinal cord that can act like a gate and either block pain messages or transmit them to the brain. Pain is experienced when pain messages carried by small, slow-conducting nerve fibers reach the gate and cause it to open. Other sensory messages from other parts of the body are carried by large, fast-conducting nerve fibers and block the pain messages at the gate. This theory also suggests that messages from the brain to the spinal cord can block the pain messages at the gate, explaining how psychological factors can influence pain perception.   Pages: 86-87

33.   Name and describe five Gestalt principles of perceptual organization.

Answer: The Gestalt psychologists argued that what we perceive is more than what we have sensed. They identified several basic principles that explain how we make sense out of the world by organizing our sensory experiences. We tend to perceive, for example, those things that have similar characteristics as belonging together, as being of one group. This is the Gestalt principle of similarity. The Gestalt principles of proximity states that things that are close together are perceived as belonging together. Closure implies that when there is a gap in an image, we tend to fill in the gap automatically. Continuity is our tendency to perceive objects as belonging together if they appear to form a continuous pattern. Finally, figure-ground states that as we view the world, an object (the figure) seems to stand out from the background (the ground).   Page: 91

1.   Chris switches on his stereo. Sound waves stimulate receptors in his ear. It is only when the signals are processed in his brain that he recognizes the sounds as the music of Metallica. This recognition by the brain is called:

Answer: (C) perception.   Page: 74

2.   Carrie purchases a new clock that chimes every hour. At first, she finds the new chime distracting, but eventually stops noticing the hourly noise. What process has taken place?

Answer: (A) sensory adaptation   Page: 75

3.   When you are complimented on the color of your eyes, which part of the eye is being noticed?

Answer: (B) the iris   Page: 76

4.   Which is the opening to the eye?

Answer: (C) the pupil   Page: 76

5.   With age, the lens loses its ability to accommodate for near vision. What is this condition called?

Answer: (D) presbyopia   Page: 76

6.   Which of the following is *not* a type of cell according to the opponent-process theory of color vision?

Answer: (C) blue/red   Page: 79

7.   The degree to which light waves producing a color are of the same wavelength is called:

Answer: (C) saturation.   Page: 78

8.   Which of the following animals can respond to sounds with the highest pitch?

Answer: (D) dolphins   Page: 81

9.   Which of the following statements best explains how we detect the location from which a sound is coming?

Answer: (B) The difference in the intensity of sound reaching each ear helps us determine location.   Page: 82

10.   Which taste sensation is triggered by the substance glutamate?

Answer: (D) umami   Page: 84

11.   Hal hurts his back while moving furniture. He realizes he has to complete the job, and while doing so, notices a reduction in pain. This is due to the activity of:

Answer: (A) endorphins.   Page: 86

12.   Viewing either a white vase or two black faces in profile in a single image is an example of:

Answer: (D) figure-ground.   Page: 91

13.   Which of the following is *not* a monocular depth cue?

Answer: (B) convergence   Page: 92

14.   If you stare at a single unmoving light in a dark room, it will appear to move. What is this phenomenon called?

Answer: (A) the autokinetic illusion   Page: 94

15.   Which of the following explains how we know that a stop sign says "stop" even if some of the letters are hidden?

Answer: (B) top-down processing   Page: 90

16.   Carla is driving across the state. She begins to focus only on the road in front of her, and she is taken by surprise when a car appears "out of nowhere" to cut her off. Which phenomenon is occurring here?

Answer: (D) inattentional blindness   Page: 88

17.   We tend to perceive objects that are close together as belonging to the same group. This illustrates the Gestalt principle of:

Answer: (C) proximity   Page: 91

18.   Many complex perceptual tasks require the brain to integrate information from more than one sense, a process called:

Answer: (A) cross-modal perception.   Page: 90

19.   The capacity for responding to stimuli with unusual perceptions along with typical ones is called:

Answer: (D) synesthesia.   Page: 97

20.   Subliminal messages are presented:

Answer: (B) below the threshold of awareness.   Page: 97

21.   The absolute threshold is the minimum amount of sensory information that can be detected 100% of the time.

Answer: False   Page: 74

22.   Sensory receptors may grow accustomed to constant, unchanging levels of stimuli over time.

Answer: True   Page: 75

23.   Rods and cones fire in sequence to encode the wavelength of light.

Answer: False   Pages: 78-79

24.   There are more cones than rods in our retina.

Answer: False   Page: 78

25.   The ossicles in the middle ear are the three smallest bones in the human body.

Answer: True   Page: 82

26.   The prevalence of chronic pain varies widely across different cultures.

Answer: True   Page: 86

27.   The kinesthetic sense provides information of the position of body parts relative to one another.

Answer: True   Page: 87

28.   A pirate wearing an eye patch over one eye would have no depth perception.

Answer: False   Page: 93

29.   Illusions occur due in part to learning.

Answer: True   Page: 95

30.   Our expectations of what we will perceive can affect our actual perceptions.

Answer: True   Page: 96

31.   Explain the two theories of color vision. Why is more than one theory needed to explain the perception of color?

Answer: Trichromatic theory explains the processing of color information at the level of the cones. It states that we have three types of color-sensitive receptors (cones), each type maximally sensitive to light of a different wavelength. This theory does not explain why we experience negative afterimages, as when staring at a green object and then looking away and seeing that same object in red. This phenomenon is explained by opponent-process theory, a theory that states that we have cells that are excited by one color and inhibited by another. The existence of cells with these properties explains why negative afterimages occur. Pages: 78-80

32.   Describe how we sense odors, including how neurons encode specific odors and their intensity.
Answer: When odor molecules vaporize, they become airborne and proceed up each nostril to the olfactory epithelium. The olfactory epithelium consists of two patches of tissue, each containing about ten million olfactory neurons, which are the sensory receptors for smell. Each neuron contains only one of the 1,000 different types of odor receptors that humans possess. Each type of odor receptor must be able to detect more than one type of odor. The intensity of the odor is determined by the number of olfactory neurons firing at the same time. Pages: 83-84

33.   Describe how you use both top-down processing and bottom-up processing when you read.

Answer: When recognizing patterns, information can be processed starting with the raw data presented or expectations and knowledge can influence what is perceived. Bottom-up processing involves developing the perception from the ground up by combining the individual components of a stimulus. In top-down processing, some information that we already have helps in the perception of the stimulus. Thus, the brain acts to influence how the incoming information is interpreted. When we have no expectations or experience with a stimulus bottom-up processing must be relied upon, while top-down processing facilitates recognition when the stimulus is familiar or information about it is provided. So when you first learn to read, or when you read an unfamiliar word, you tend to sound out a word one letter or sound at a time, which is bottom-up processing. When you read a passage from a book, containing words and ideas with which you are familiar, you use top-down processing, because you don't need to focus on each individual word so much as the overall meaning of the passage.   Page: 90

1.   A mental state other than wakefulness, such as sleep or meditation is called:

Answer: (C) altered state of consciousness.   Page: 110

2.   Circadian rhythms exist for:

Answer: (D) all of the above.   Page: 110

3.   Which hormone is most related to the sleep/wake cycle?

Answer: (C) melatonin.   Page: 110

4.   _____ occurs in four stages.

Answer: (D) NREM sleep   Page: 111

5.   Which EEG pattern is typical of someone who is relaxed and drowsy, but not yet asleep?

Answer: (A) alpha waves   Page: 112

6.   Jonas stayed up all night at a party. The next night when he slept, he had nightmares. This was probably because of:

Answer: (B) REM rebound effect.   Page: 112

7.   Which theory best explains the function of sleep in humans?

Answer: (C) a combination of both the restorative and circadian theories of sleep   Page: 114

8.   Laura describes a dream she had to her friend, Jessica. Jessica explains her view of what the dream means. Jessica is offering her opinion of what aspect of Laura's dream?

Answer: (B) the latent content   Page: 117

9.   Which of the following best describes the activation-synthesis hypothesis of dreaming?

Answer: (D) Dreams are the brain's attempt to make sense of the random firing of brain cells during REM sleep.   Page: 117

10.   The technical term for talking in one's sleep is:

Answer: (A) somniloquy.   Page: 117

11.   Which of the following major sleep disorders may be treated through surgery?

Answer: (B) sleep apnea   Page: 118

12.   Nightmares and sleep terrors:

Answer: (A) occur during different stages of sleep.   Page: 117

13.   Terrell spends time every morning sitting alone, quietly concentrating on the sound of his own breathing. He says that 20 minutes of quiet time like this clear his mind and cause him to feel rested and alert. Terrell is experiencing the benefits of:

Answer: (D) meditation.   Pages: 118-119

14.   Which of the following statements about hypnosis is true?

Answer: (C) People are more suggestible while hypnotized.   Page: 120

15.   Which theory of hypnosis posits that the behavior of a hypnotized person is a function of their own expectations about how people behave while hypnotized?

Answer: (A) the sociocognitive theory of hypnosis   Page: 120

16.   Which of the following is *not* a psychoactive drug?

Answer: (D) all of the above are psychoactive drugs   Page: 122

17.   Alcohol is classified as a:

Answer: (D) depressant.   Page: 122

18.   Blake uses cocaine. He finds he needs more cocaine now to receive the same effect he once received from smaller amounts of the drug. This symptom of cocaine dependence is called:

Answer: (C) drug tolerance.   Pages: 123-124

19.   At what point does casual use of a psychoactive drug become abuse?

Answer: (C) when use of the drug has begun to negatively affect important aspects of the person's life and functioning.   Page: 122

20.   The neurotransmitter associated with the feelings of reward or pleasure produced by many psychoactive substances is:

Answer: (B) dopamine.   Page: 122

21.   Chronic jet lag can result in permanent memory deficits.

Answer: True   Page: 110

22.   Exposure to bright sunlight during early morning hours and voidance of bright light in the evening may help restore circadian rhythms.

Answer: True   Page: 110

23.   Sleep deprivation may negatively affect mood, but has little affect on cognitive performance.

Answer: False   Page: 114

24.   Dreams only occur during REM sleep.

Answer: False   Page: 115

25.   Chronic insomnia can last for years, and affects about 10% of all adults.

Answer: True   Page: 118

26.   Meditation has been shown to help some people with depression.

Answer: True   Page: 119

27.   Hypnosis has been effective in helping patients control pain.

Answer: True   Page: 120

28.   Substance abuse is a more severe problem than substance dependence.

Answer: False   Page: 123

29.   An individual addicted to cocaine who tries to quit using will often feel nervous and hyper.

Answer: False   Page: 125

30. Marijuana has been associated with apathy and a decline in school performance.

Answer: True   Page: 127

31. Describe the progression through the various stages of the sleep cycle, including the EEG pattern typical of each stage.

Answer: There are four NREM stages of sleep: Stages 1, 2, 3, and 4. Stage 1 is the lightest stage of sleep and Stage 4 is the deepest. REM sleep, characterized by rapid eye movements, an active brain, and inhibition of the large muscles of the body, is the fifth stage of sleep. Throughout the night, sleep cycles progress from Stage 1 through Stage 4 and then back down to Stage 2. From Stage 2 you progress into REM sleep, instead of back to Stage 1. After the first two full sleep cycles, the pattern changes and most sleep time is spent alternating between Stage 2 and REM sleep. As the night goes on, more time is spent in REM sleep. Each stage of sleep has a characteristic pattern of brain wave activity as indicated by EEG. Stage 1 sleep is characterized by small, irregular brain patterns and some alpha waves. In Stage 2 the typical pattern is that of sleep spindles. By Stage 3, delta waves appear, and Stage 4 is characterized by mostly delta waves.   Pages: 112-113

32. Distinguish between the dream theories of Freud and Hobson.

Answer: Freud believed that dreaming was a means of expressing unacceptable wishes or impulses. He thought that these unacceptable desires were expressed symbolically so as not to upset the dreamer. The dream as it was recalled is the manifest content and the true meaning behind the dream is the latent content. A very different explanation of dreaming is Hobson's activation-synthesis hypothesis. This proposes that dreams occur because the brain is trying to make sense of the random firing of brain cells that occurs during REM sleep. From the random activity (activation), a story is synthesized.   Pages: 116-117

33.   Distinguish between the general effects of stimulants, depressants, and hallucinogens, including the typical pattern of withdrawal symptoms for each.

Answer: Stimulants speed up activity in the central nervous system, suppress appetite, and can make a person feel more awake, alert, and energetic. Stimulants increase pulse rate, blood pressure, and respiration rate, and reduce cerebral blood flow. Withdrawal symptoms for different stimulants may include fatigue, long periods of sleep, depression, anxiety, and increased irritability. Depressants decrease activity in the central nervous system, slow down bodily functions, and reduce sensitivity to outside stimulation. Withdrawal symptoms for different depressants may include anxiety, nausea, irritability, muscle tension, tremors, or cramps, sleeping problems, and in some cases severe and life-threatening physiological difficulties. Hallucinogens alter or distort the perception of time and space, alter mood, and produce feelings of unreality. Hallucinogens tend to magnify the mood of the user at the time the drug is taken, and tend to hamper creative thinking. Withdrawal symptoms for different hallucinogens may include anxiety, depression, fatigue, decreased appetite, and hyperactivity.
Pages: 122-124, 128

1.   An awareness of one's own thoughts, feelings, perceptions, sensations and external environment is called:

Answer: (C) consciousness.   Page: 110

2.   Which of the following is not considered an altered state of consciousness?

Answer: (A) wakefulness   Page: 110

3.   The biological clock that controls circadian rhythms is the:

Answer: (A) suprachiasmatic nucleus.   Page: 110

4.   Manny has worked the night shift at his job for some time. He sometimes has to run errands for his family during the day, and he finds himself being less attentive and with a slower reaction time when he does so. This time period of reduced attention and efficiency is called:

Answer: (D) subjective night.   Page: 110

5.   During which stage of sleep are you likely to find an EEG pattern of sleep spindles?

Answer: (B) stage 2   Page: 113

6.   The typical sleep cycle lasts approximately:

Answer: (B) 90 minutes.   Page: 113

7.   Which of the following is *not* a characteristic of REM sleep?

Answer: (D) movement of the limbs   Page: 111

8.   About half of a full night's sleep is spent in what stage?

Answer: (C) stage 4   Page: 113

9.   Which theory of sleep is consistent with evolutionary theory?

Answer: (B) circadian theory of sleep   Page: 114

10.   Who suggested that dreams are symbolic representations of unconscious urges and desires?

Answer: (D) Sigmund Freud   Pages: 116-117

11.   Somnambulism, or sleepwalking, occurs during a partial arousal from which stage of sleep?

Answer: (C) stage 4   Page: 117

12.   Narcolepsy:

Answer: (C) can be treated with stimulants.   Page: 118

13.   Which of the following is *not* a potential health benefit of meditation?

Answer: (B) burning fat cells   Page: 119

14.   Which theory suggests that hypnosis induces a split between two aspects of the control of consciousness?

Answer: (C) neodissociation   Pages: 120-121

15.   What percentage of people can reach the deepest levels of the hypnotized state?

Answer: (A) 5%   Page: 120

16.   Ways of inducing altered states are found in _____ cultures.

Answer: (D) all   Page: 121

17.   Depressants have a calming, sedating effect by working on receptors for which neurotransmitter?

Answer: (A) GABA   Page: 122

18.   Physical dependence is characterized by _____ & _____.

Answer: (A) tolerance; withdrawal   Pages: 123-124

19.   A class of depressants derived from the opium poppy, offering pain-relieving effects are:

Answer: (D) narcotics.   Page: 126

20.   Psychoactive substances produce a pleasurable effect by acting on which part of the limbic system of the brain?

Answer: (D) the nucleus accumbens   Page: 122

21.   An altered state of consciousness involves a change in awareness.

Answer: True   Page: 110

22.   NREM dreams are less frequent and memorable than REM dreams.

Answer: True   Page: 115

23.   REM sleep is the stage we reach our deepest sleep.

Answer: False   Page: 113

24.   During lucid dreams the individual is aware they are dreaming and able to influence the dream.

Answer: True   Page: 116

25.   Sleep terrors are more vivid than nightmares, and are more likely to keep the dreamer awake afterward.

Answer: False   Page: 117

26.   Even staying up a bit later on Friday and Saturday nights can negatively impact one's mood on Monday morning.

Answer: True   Page: 114

27.   A hypnotized person is under the complete control of the hypnotist.

Answer: False   Page: 120

28.   Opiates mimic the body's own endorphins and thus are useful in pain management.

Answer: True   Page: 122

29.   Alcohol serves to make men more aggressive, sexually aroused, and able to perform sexually.

Answer: False   Page: 126

30.   Marijuana can be best classified as a hallucinogen.

Answer: True   Page: 127

31. Name and describe four parasomnias.

Answer: Parasomnias are sleep disturbances in which behaviors and physical states that normally occur only in the waking state take place during sleep. Sleepwalking, or somnambulism, occurs during a partial arousal from stage 4 sleep in which the sleeper does not come to full consciousness. Somniloquy, or sleeptalking, can occur in any stage, and usually involves mumbling of nonsensical words and phrases. Sleep terrors happen during stage 4 sleep. The sleeper screams, then awakens in a panic with their eyes open, heart pounding, perspiring, and breathing rapidly. Typically, the individual falls back to sleep quickly. Nightmares occur during REM sleep and are thus more vivid, and more likely to be recalled, as the sleeper awakens to full consciousness.   Pages: 117-118

32. Review the three theories of hypnosis.

Answer: Each of the three theories of hypnosis provides a different explanation for the behavior of a hypnotized person. According to the sociocognitive theory, hypnotized individuals are behaving as they think good hypnotized subjects should; they are playing the role of a hypnotized person according to their expectations. The neodissociation theory sees the hypnotized state as the result of a dissociation, a separation of different aspects of consciousness: planning element and the monitoring function. The theory of dissociated control says that the hypnotized subject has given over control of his or her behavior and is responding automatically to the directions of the hypnotist. There is some support for each of these, but many questions about hypnosis remain unanswered.   Pages: 120-121

33. Distinguish between physical and psychological drug dependence.

Answer: Substance abuse occurs when the use of a drug is interfering with one's life. The drug use may be having a negative impact on work, family, or other important parts of one's life. Physical drug dependence has developed when drug use has caused the body to adapt to the presence of the drug; therefore, more drug is needed to get the desired effect (tolerance) and withdrawal symptoms are seen when the drug is no longer present. Both tolerance and withdrawal demonstrate that the body is compensating for the effects of the drug. Psychological dependence can occur with or without physical dependence and is characterized by craving and a psychological need for the drug. Learning and other environmental factors are involved in the development of psychological dependence. Such factors need to be addressed in order to effectively treat drug problems.   Pages: 123-124

1.   The individual most directly responsible for the process of classical conditioning is:

Answer: (B) Ivan Pavlov.   Page: 138

2.   Billy's father always yells at him to "come here now" before administering a spanking. Billy begins to cry when his father yells that phrase at him. In this example of classical conditioning, which is the *conditioned stimulus*?

Answer: (C) Billy's father's yell of "come here now"   Page: 139

3.   The weakening and eventual disappearance of a conditioned response that is caused by repeated presentation of the conditioned stimulus without the presence of the unconditioned stimulus is called:

Answer: (D) extinction.   Page: 140

4.   The type of classical conditioning that accounts for learning when conditioned stimuli are linked together to form a series of signals is called:

Answer: (C) higher-order conditioning.   Page: 140

5.   Jerry bought a dog specifically to serve as a watch dog. He teaches his dog to bark whenever the door bell rings. However, the dog also barks at the telephone or a door bell rung on television. Which process explains these additional responses?

Answer: (C) generalization   Page: 140

6.   John B. Watson's work with "little Albert" was significant because it demonstrated:

Answer: (A) a conditioned fear response.   Page: 142

7.   Janie once ate fish at a restaurant and later felt ill. Now the very smell of cooked fish makes her nauseous. What has Janie experienced?

Answer: (B) a taste aversion   Page: 144

8.   Bill completes his drug rehabilitation program. His counselor strongly urges him to avoid going to places where he used to use drugs. His counselor, knowledgeable about classical conditioning, says this so that:

Answer: (D) Bill doesn't come into contact with stimuli previously associated with drug use.
        Page: 145

9.   Thorndike's experiments using the cat who had to learn to escape the puzzle box for food illustrated which behavioral law?

Answer: (C) law of effect   Pages: 145-146

10.   Which of the following is the clearest example of operant conditioning?

Answer: (D) a dog sits because it has previously been given a treat for sitting.   Page: 146

11.   The process of shaping a response involves reinforcing each of a series of steps which are more and more similar to the desired response. This process thus relies on:

Answer: (A) successive approximations.   Page: 150

12.   What causes extinction in operant conditioning?

Answer: (B) withholding reinforcement   Page: 150

13.   Cindy cries for candy when in the store with her mother. Her mother, wanting Cindy to be quiet, gives in and gets her some candy, at which point Cindy silences. The next time they go to the store, the process repeats itself. Which of the following best describes what has happened?

Answer: (B) Cindy's behavior is positively reinforced, and her mother's behavior is negatively reinforced.   Page: 147

14.   A stoplight uses different colors to trigger different behaviors: green for go, red for stop. This is most similar to which concept in operant conditioning?

Answer: (C) discriminative stimulus   Page: 150

15.   Which of the following is the best example of a primary reinforcer?

Answer: (C) water   Page: 147

16.   A professor gives his class a quiz each Monday. Consequently, students do not study much during the week, but "cram" through the weekend in order to earn a good grade. Their behavior best corresponds to which schedule of reinforcement?

Answer: (C) fixed interval   Page: 148

17.   When Billy misbehaves, his parents make sure to apply punishment immediately, and consistently, and to use the harshest possible punishment so that Billy will "get the message." Which of the following is a recommendation you might make to help their use of punishment be more effective?

Answer: (A) make punishment less severe   Page: 152

18.   Seligman's experiments with dogs who did not escape the shock administered, even when they could have, demonstrates which principle?

Answer: (B) learned helplessness   Page: 153

19.   Carrie is trying to complete a jigsaw puzzle. She has struggled with it for some time until she suddenly sees how the pieces fit together. Which type of learning is Carrie exhibiting?

Answer: (A) insight learning   Page: 156

20.   Carl learns how to change a flat tire by watching his mom do so. She would change a tire, and then have him show her each step as well. Which type of learning does this demonstrate?

Answer: (D) a modeling effect   Page: 158

21.   Memorizing a phone number long enough to dial it, and then forgetting it, fits the text definition of learning.

Answer: False   Page: 137

22.   Classical conditioning occurs most readily when the unconditioned stimulus occurs just before the conditioned stimulus.

Answer: False   Page: 143

23.   John B. Watson coined the term "behaviorism" for the school that proposed limiting psychology to the study of overtly observable behavior.

Answer: True   Page: 142

24.   The cognitive view of classical conditioning suggests that the repeated pairing of the conditioned stimulus and unconditioned stimulus is the critical element for conditioning to occur.

Answer: False   Page: 143

25.   The "operant" in operant conditioning refers to a voluntary behavior.

Answer: True   Page: 146

26.   The partial reinforcement effect occurs when reinforcement is intermittent and learning proceeds more quickly.

Answer: False   Page: 148

27.   Punishment can suppress behavior, but not extinguish it.

Answer: True   Page: 151

28.   Biofeedback can be used to train individuals to control internal responses such as heart rate and brain-wave pattern.

Answer: True   Page: 154

29.   Behavior modification programs require a therapist to administer them.

Answer: False   Page: 154

30.   The process of latent learning depends upon reinforcement taking place.

Answer: False   Page: 156

31.   Distinguish between the process of extinction in classical conditioning, and the process of extinction in operant conditioning.

Answer: In classical conditioning, extinction represents the weakening and eventual disappearance of the conditioned response as a result of repeated presentation of the conditioned stimulus without the unconditioned stimulus. In operant conditioning, extinction represents the weakening and eventual disappearance of a response as a result of the withholding of reinforcement. So in both forms of learning, a response is weakened and disappears, but extinction occurs due to different processes in each form of learning.   Pages: 140, 150

32.   Design a reinforcement plan to teach your dog to roll over. Include the type of reinforcement used, schedule of reinforcement, and why you chose those in particular.

Answer: A dog is unlikely to spontaneously roll over, much less to do so on command the first time. In order to teach a dog this complex behavior, you can reinforce approximations of the desired behavior, an application called shaping. You might, for example, reward the dog for sitting. Then you would reward it for lying down. You might need to encourage the dog by pressing on his backside to get him to sit, or to get him to roll over by holding the treat as he lies down so that he must reach for it and tumble. To first train him to roll over, every response of rolling over should be rewarded. Later, an intermittent reinforcement schedule, such as a variable ratio schedule, will maintain the behavior at a high rate yet keep it resistant to extinction.
Pages: 146-149

33.   Describe Bandura's "Bobo Doll" study and its implications for television violence.

Answer: Albert Bandura conducted a study on the process of observational learning, or learning through modeling, as a means of children learning aggressive behaviors. One classic study involved preschoolers. One group of children observed an adult model punching, kicking, and hitting a 5-foot, inflated plastic "Bobo Doll," a second group observed a nonaggressive model who ignored the Bobo Doll and played quietly with other toys, while a third group was a control group did not observe a model. Later, each child was observed playing, and children exposed to the aggressive model imitated much of the aggression they witnessed, and engaged in more nonimitative aggression than did children in the other groups. The implications of this study are that children may engage in increased levels of aggressive behavior when viewing such actions on television.   Page: 159

1.   A baby develops the skill of walking. Why is it *not* appropriate, according to the text's definition of learning, to say she *learned* to walk?

Answer: (B) Walking occurs due to maturation.   Page: 137

2.   Linda remembers the first time her boy friend kissed her. A certain song was on the radio at the time, and her heart was racing. Now, whenever Linda hears that same song, her heart starts racing. In this example of classical conditioning, which is the *conditioned response*?

Answer: (D) Linda's heart racing when the song plays   Page: 139

3.   Which term refers to the reappearance of an extinguished response in a weaker form when an organism is exposed to the original conditioned stimulus following a rest period?

Answer: (A) spontaneous recovery   Page: 140

4.   Blinking after hearing a word that has previously been paired with a puff of air at your eye is known as a:

Answer: (D) conditioned reflex.   Page: 138

5.   In your text, Little Albert is described as becoming afraid of a rabbit and a fur coat. This fact demonstrates the phenomenon known as:

Answer: (B) generalization   Page: 140

6.   Which individual is responsible for the work on the conditioned fear response with "Little Albert"?

Answer: (C) John B. Watson   Page: 142

7.   What makes taste aversion an exception to the basic rules of classical conditioning?

Answer: (A) The effect appears after only one pairing.   Page: 144

8.   Classical conditioning appears to occur more rapidly when a stimulus has "ecological relevance." This refers to:

Answer: (A) the idea that a neutral stimulus must have some authentic connection to the unconditioned stimulus.   Page: 145

9.   You want to teach your dog to sit on command. If you plan to give your dog a special treat when he sits, knowing that such a reward will likely make the dog respond to your command to sit more often. How do you get your dog to sit the first time so that you can reward him for it?

Answer: (C) by reinforcing successive approximations   Page: 150

10.   Anything that causes an increase in a target behavior is a:

Answer: (A) reinforcer.   Page: 146

11.   Cindy cries for candy when in the store with her mother. Her mother, wanting Cindy to be quiet, gives in and gets her some candy, at which point Cindy silences. The next time they go to the store, the process repeats itself. Which of the following best describes what has happened?

Answer: (B) Cindy's behavior is positively reinforced, and her mother's behavior is negatively reinforced.   Page: 147

12.   What causes extinction in operant conditioning?

Answer: (B) withholding reinforcement   Page: 150

13.   Which of the following is a secondary reinforcer?

Answer: (C) money   Page: 147

14.   Police cars in your area are blue. When you see a police car while you are driving, you automatically take your foot off of the gas pedal. You do not behave the same way when you see other blue vehicles because the police car is actually a:

Answer: (D) discriminative stimulus   Page: 150

15.   The highest response rates occur with which reinforcement schedule?

Answer: (C) variable ratio   Page: 148

16.   Someone with a fear of elevators always takes the stairs; this behavior occurs due to:

Answer: (B) negative reinforcement.   Page: 147

17.   Jerry's class uses a system whereby points are earned for appropriate behaviors such as doing homework, sitting quietly, and participating well in class activities. The points can be exchanged for tangible rewards such as not having to do homework or an extra recess period. Which behavior modification technique does Jerry's class seem to be using?

Answer: (C) token economy   Page: 154

18.   Carrie is trying to complete a jigsaw puzzle. She has struggled with it for some time until she suddenly sees how the pieces fit together. Which type of learning is Carrie exhibiting?

Answer: (A) insight learning   Page: 156

19.   Who conducted the famous "Bobo Doll" study that demonstrated that children could learn aggressive behavior through observational learning?

Answer: (C) Albert Bandura   Page: 159

20.   Kyle has been told by his parents that he shouldn't smoke because it's unhealthy. He watches a movie in which his favorite action star smokes while looking healthy and beating up bad guys. The next day, Kyle begins smoking. The movie he saw had:

Answer: (C) a disinhibitory effect   Page: 158

21.   Under certain conditions, a conditioned response can occur to an unconditioned stimulus.

Answer: False   Page: 139

22.   Spontaneous recovery can only occur once a response has been extinguished.

Answer: True   Page: 140

23.   In Watson's work with Little Albert, the white rat was the conditioned stimulus.

Answer: True   Page: 142

24.   Classical conditioning can affect the responses of internal organs.

Answer: True   Pages: 143-144

25.   Negative reinforcement increases the probability of a response.

Answer: True   Page: 147

26.   Skinner is known for his work with hungry cats and "puzzle boxes."

Answer: False   Page: 146

27.   Generalization and discrimination are seen in both classical and operant conditioning.

Answer: True   Pages: 140-141, 150

28.   Fixed schedules of reinforcement are more resistant to extinction than are variable schedules of reinforcement.

Answer: False   Pages: 147-148

29.   The more severe a punishment is, the more effective it is.

Answer: False   Page: 151

30.   Solutions gained by insight are more easily learned and remembered than are solutions learned by rote memorization.

Answer: True   Page: 156

31.   Describe how the cognitive view of classical conditioning differs from that of Pavlov.

Answer: Pavlov viewed classical conditioning as a mechanical and automatic process. He believed that if two stimuli were presented in the appropriate way, conditioning would necessarily occur. Pavlov did not recognize that there are limits to what can be conditioned. Contemporary views of classical conditioning find fault with Pavlov's view. In order for conditioning to occur, the conditioned stimulus must reliably predict the unconditioned stimulus. Page: 143

32.   Design a program of punishment to prevent a child from engaging in a dangerous behavior, such as playing with electrical cords. Discuss how the punishment program meets the recommendations in the text for making punishment more effective.

Answer: Punishment involves the removal of a pleasant stimulus or the application of an unpleasant stimulus, thus lowering the probability of a response. In general, punishment has disadvantages, but in the case of a dangerous behavior such as a child playing with electrical cords, its use may be warranted. Ideally, punishment in such a situation should be applied as soon as the child approaches or touches the cords, in order to prevent the behavior from being rewarding. In this case, a stern "no!" followed, only if necessary, by a swat on the wrist or hand, of just enough severity to suppress the behavior. Finally, the punishment should be applied every single time the child approaches or attempts to touch the electrical cords.   Pages: 151-152

33.   Describe how you might use the process of shaping to teach a rat to press a lever in a Skinner box.

Answer: Shaping is a process for teaching a complex behavior that may not naturally appear. This application of operant conditioning is used when training animals. You might first reward the rat for looking ay or approaching the lever, then for touching the lever with a paw, and finally for pressing down on the lever. Behaviors that are similar to the desired behavior are reinforced as the animal gets closer and closer to performing the desired response.   Pages: 147-150

1.   Any steps you take to try to commit something to memory are part of the _____ process.

Answer: (B) encoding   Page: 170

2.   When you call information for a phone number, but you don't have a pen to write down the number, what part of your memory must attempt to maintain the number while you run around looking for a pen?

Answer: (C) short term memory   Page: 171

3.   The strategy of grouping bits of information into larger units that are easier to remember is called:

Answer: (D) chunking.   Page: 171

4.   In order for information in long-term memory to be used, it must be:

Answer: (C) retrieved.   Page: 173

5.   Memories of a vacation spent with your family would be considered:

Answer: (B) episodic memories.   Page: 173

6.   Which of the following is not one of the three types of nondeclarative memories?

Answer: (A) information learned in class   Page: 173

7.   A memory researcher asks subjects to memorize a list of words, and finds it takes them 30 minutes to do so. Two weeks later, he asks them to memorize the list of words again, and they do so in 15 minutes. The percentage of time saved, 50%, is known as the:

Answer: (A) savings score.   Page: 174

8.   An integrated framework about people, objects and events which is stored in long term memory is called a:

Answer: (B) schema.   Page: 174

9.   Henry is in college, and he has difficulty remembering events from the first few years of his life. This is due to:

Answer: (C) infantile amnesia, and quite normal.   Page: 178

10.   There is a good chance that you remember exactly where you were and what you were doing when you first heard about the attacks on September 11, 2001. Such a vivid memory is called a _____ memory.

Answer: (A) flashbulb   Page: 179

11.   According to the serial position effect, which items on a list are *least* likely to be recalled?

Answer: (B) the middle few   Page: 181

12.   Vern has too much to drink at a party. The next day he gets a phone call from a woman he met at the party, but he does not remember her name. According to the state-dependent memory effect, under which condition is Vern most likely to remember her name?

Answer: (D) when he is drunk   Page: 182

13.   The physiological process responsible for the formation of memories is called:

Answer: (B) long-term potentiation.   Page: 184

14.   Which of the following hormones has *not* been related to memory processes, according to your text?

Answer: (C) testosterone   Pages: 184-185

15.   Jacquez believes that as you get older, memories that haven't been used will just fade away and disappear. His position is most consistent with which cause of forgetting?

Answer: (A) decay theory   Page: 186

16.   David studied French in high school, but switched to learning Italian in college. Whenever he tries to speak French, he catches himself instead translating his English phrases into Italian. Why is David forgetting his French?

Answer: (C) retroactive interference   Page: 187

17.   Which of the following is not a form of motivated forgetting?

Answer: (D) retrograde amnesia   Page: 188

18.   Cassie is playing Trivial Pursuit with friends. Whenever she is asked a question, she gets frustrated because insists she knows the answer but can't seem to remember it. What is Cassie experiencing?

Answer: (B) the tip-of-the-tongue phenomenon   Page: 189

19.   Another name for "cramming" - generally considered less effective than other methods, is:

Answer: (C) massed practice.   Page: 189

20.   ROYGBIV, an acronym representing the colors of the visual spectrum, is a type of:

Answer: (D) mnemonic device.   Page: 191

21.   Elaborative rehearsal is the best method for remembering complex information like material for this class.

Answer: True   Page: 172

22.   Recall tasks are typically considered to be easier than recognition tasks.

Answer: False   Page: 173

23.   A reconstruction of an event may be based on inaccurate information.

Answer: True   Pages: 174-175

24.   Eyewitness testimony is reliable evidence in criminal court cases.

Answer: False   Page: 176

25.   Human memory abilities can be significantly enhanced in certain cultures.

Answer: False   Page: 180

26.   Your strongest, most long-lasting memories are usually those fueled by your emotions.

Answer: True   Page: 182

27.   Hermann Ebbinghaus conducted the first experimental studies on learning and memory.

Answer: True   Page: 185

28.   Studying similar subjects decreases the amount of interference experienced.

Answer: False   Page: 187

29.   Overlearning involves studying so hard you can't remember what you studied.

Answer: False   Page: 189

30.   Engaging in spaced practice will help you remember more in less study time.

Answer: True   Page: 189

31.   Describe the "reconstructive" nature of memory, including the impact of schemas and positive bias.

Answer: Memory is not a "snapshot" of an event, but an account of an event that has been pieced together from a few highlights, using information that may or may not be accurate. Memories are recreations, with remembered material supplemented with details that fit expectations or beliefs. As such, schemas, which are frameworks of knowledge and assumptions we have about people, objects, and events, influence our memories. We are more likely to recall, or even create, details that are consistent with our schemas. Positive bias is a distortion of autobiographical memories, in that we are more likely to remember pleasant events than unpleasant ones, and to distort unpleasant memories so that they become more pleasant over time.   Pages: 174-176

32.   What is long-term potentiation, and how is it related to learning?

Answer: Long-term potentiation (LTP) is a strengthening of neuronal transmission at a synapse that lasts for at least several hours and is thought to be the physiological process that is behind the formation of memories. This assertion is supported by research that demonstrates that blocking LTP disrupts or prevents some forms of learning.   Pages: 184

33.   Describe a plan for studying that incorporates four recommendations from your text to improve your memory.

Answer: Organizing information when encoding can facilitate retrieval. Organization is a strategy one can use by writing out headings and subheadings of text material or class notes. One can even integrate the two into one organized set of notes so that studying from each source isn't seen as a separate project. Overlearning is a strategy that involves practicing or studying material beyond the point where it can be repeated once without error. So when trying to memorize a definition or list of terms, instead of stopping with one error-free repetition from memory, continuing to study and recite the material will lead to superior and more long-term retrieval. If one typically engages in cramming, or massed practice, which involves trying to learn in a long session without rest, it might be better to try spaced practice. Spaced practice involves using shorter study periods broken up with breaks between each period. Finally, using recitation involves closing one's eyes and seeing how much of the information can be repeated aloud from memory.   Pages: 189-191

1.   The act of maintaining information in the memory is called:

Answer: (B) storage.   Page: 170

2.   Your instructor suggests that when you study, you should relate psychological concepts to events you have encountered in your day-to-day life. She is encouraging you to engage in:

Answer: (B) elaborative rehearsal.   Page: 172

3.   Which of the following memory systems holds information for as little as a fraction of a second?

Answer: (A) sensory memory   Page: 170

4.   As you read these questions, you most likely use the _____ part of your memory in order to answer correctly.

Answer: (A) semantic   Page: 173

5.   What type of memory task is involved in answering fill-in-the-blank questions?

Answer: (D) recall   Page: 173

6.   Trying to remember a phone number by repeating it over and over again is called:

Answer: (A) maintenance rehearsal.   Page: 172

7.   Sometimes erroneous information is supplied to an eyewitness after an event is over. This can affect the accuracy of eyewitnesses' recollections -- a phenomenon called the:

Answer: (C) misinformation effect.   Page: 176

8.   Which of the following events is least likely to be considered a "flashbulb" memory?

Answer: (C) eating your breakfast this morning   Page: 179

9.   Research on childhood memories has demonstrated that:

Answer: (B) simply imagining experiences can lead to false memories.   Page: 177

10.   Why does your text suggest people of various cultures can perform unique and amazing memory tasks?

Answer: (C) People of all cultures are better able to remember that which matters to them.
        Page: 180

11.   You may find that you perform better on exams if you study in the same room in which you will later take the test according to the:

Answer: (C) context-dependent memory effect.   Page: 181

12.   Which region is responsible for many of the functions necessary for episodic and semantic memory?

Answer: (D) hippocampal   Page: 182

13.   The inability to form long-term memories following a brain injury is called:

Answer: (D) anterograde amnesia.   Pages: 182-183

14.   Which of the following statements regarding hormones and memory is *false*:

Answer: (A) Estrogen and progesterone decrease risk of dementia in postmenopausal women.
        Pages: 184-185

15.   You know how to play the flute but decide to learn to play the clarinet, unfortunately, you have trouble because you keep trying the same finger positions you would use for the flute! Your previous experience is interfering with your attempt to learn something new. Your text calls this:

Answer: (D) proactive interference.   Page: 187

16.   The researcher who studied memory using lists of nonsense syllables was

Answer: (B) Ebbinghaus.   Page: 185

17.   Lonnie is struggling in school. He meets with his professor and tells her about his study habits, which seem to be ineffective. She suggests that he try studying differently, and that his difficulty remembering material on the exams is due to:

Answer: (A) encoding failure.   Page: 186

18.   Jessica hates going to the dentist, and she completely forgot about her last appointment. This is an example of:

Answer: (C) prospective forgetting.   Page: 188

19.   Studying by reading material and then closing your eyes to see how much you can recall is called:

Answer: (A) recitation.   Page: 190

20.   Which of the following is *not* a type of mnemonic device?

Answer: (B) the repetition method   Page: 191

21.   Chunking is a strategy that increases the capacity of sensory memory.

Answer: False   Page: 171

22.   Research indicates that the two types of declarative memory function independently.

Answer: False   Page: 173

23.   Remembering how to drive your car is a nondeclarative memory.

Answer: True   Page: 173

24.   Long-term potentiation is a temporary decrease in the strength of neuronal firing.

Answer: False   Page: 184

25.   According to both the primary and recency effects, you are least likely to recall items in the middle of a sequence.

Answer: True   Page: 181

26.   Memories with significant emotional impact activate the amygdala.

Answer: True   Page: 184

27.   The process of consolidation is most related to the process of memory retrieval.

Answer: False   Page: 187

28. Schemas may both aid and distort memory.

Answer: True   Page: 175

29. The more certain a witness is of his/her testimony; the more likely it is to be accurate.

Answer: False   Page: 176

30. Mnemonic devices only help you remember things for a short period of time.

Answer: False   Page: 191

31. Define elaborative rehearsal and explain how it facilitates learning.

Answer: Elaborative rehearsal involves relating an item to be learned to knowledge you already possess. Instead of just memorizing a definition, for example, you should try to relate the definition to something you already know. Whenever an instructor asks you to apply a course concept to yourself, she or he is encouraging you to use this technique. The more you relate course concepts to yourself, the more likely it is that they will be stored in long-term memory and that you will be able to retrieve the information when it is needed.   Pages: 172

32. Describe the controversy surrounding recovered repressed memories.

Answer: A debate rages over reports from individuals in therapy who claim to have "recovered" memories of being abused as children after being unaware of such abuse for most of their lives. Suggestions made in the book, *The Courage to Heal*, included the idea that if a person cannot recall a specific instance of abuse, but still has a feeling that they suffered abuse at one time, then abuse probably did occur. Many psychologists are skeptical about such "recovered" memories, in part due to the reconstructive nature of memory. These psychologists argue that the "memories" of abuse are created by the suggestions of therapists. Most do not believe that all such instances of recovered memories are false, but that such recovered memories of abuse are rare. One reason for this skepticism is that the hippocampus, which is vital for the formation of episodic memories, is not fully developed in the first few years of life.   Pages: 177-179

33. Describe the forms of motivated forgetting.

Answer: Motivated forgetting is forgetting through suppression or repression in order to protect oneself from material that is painful, frightening, or otherwise unpleasant. One form of such forgetting is suppression, in which a person makes a conscious, active attempt to put a painful, disturbing, anxiety- or guilt-provoking memory out of mind, but the person is still aware that the event occurred. Repression is similar, except that the painful memory is literally removed from consciousness, and the person is no longer aware that the unpleasant event ever occurred. Finally, prospective forgetting involves not remembering to carry out some intended action, typically a task that is seen as unimportant, unpleasant, or burdensome.   Pages: 188

1.   Acquiring, storing, retrieving and using information, based on sensation, perception, problem solving and conceptualizing is called:.

Answer: (C) cognition.   Page: 201

2.   Which of the following would *not* be considered a concept?

Answer: (B) your dog Spike   Page: 201

3.   Individual instances of a concept that are stored in memory from personal experience are called:

Answer: (D) exemplars.   Page: 202

4.   Which of the following is the most likely prototype of a bird?

Answer: (A) a sparrow   Page: 202

5.   You are trying to decide what kind of breakfast cereal to buy. You notice a new cereal that you recall seeing advertised on television and choose to buy it. The kind of decision making fits best with the concept of the:

Answer: (B) recognition heuristic   Page: 203

6.   A cognitive rule of thumb, _____ says that the probability of an event or the importance it is given is based on its existence in prior memory.

Answer: (D) availability heuristic   Page: 203

7.   Kayla is playing blackjack and has a hand totaling 17. She knows chances are good that she will lose if she chooses to get another card but she does so anyway because she has a "gut feeling" she will get a lucky card. On what is Kayla's decision-making based?

Answer: (C) intuition   Page: 205

8.   When you learn a specific procedure for solving a math problem that will always lead you to the correct answer, you are learning a(n)

Answer: (C) algorithm.   Page: 206

9.   Juanita visits her adviser at college and afterward figures out when she will graduate by counting how many classes she has left and determining how many terms it will take to complete them. She is using:

Answer: (B) means-end analysis.   Page: 205

10.   _____leads to the tendency to apply a familiar strategy to the solution of a problem without carefully considering the special requirements of the problem.

Answer: (D) your mental set.   Page: 206

11.   How many phonemes are in the word "psychology"?

Answer: (C) 8   Page: 208

12.   Intonation and social rules are part of which component of language?

Answer: (B) pragmatics   Page: 208

13.   The language you think largely determines the nature of your thoughts. This is:

Answer: (D) linguistic relativity hypothesis.   Page: 210

14.   Thurston believed there are seven distinct capabilities that are involved in all intellectual activities, and he referred to these as:

Answer: (A) primary mental abilities.   Page: 213

15.   Wes is a con artist who flunked out of school and is unemployed but runs "scams" to earn his living. He has played a bum, a cop, a priest, and a businessman as part of his efforts to cheat people, and he has never been caught. Wes likely would score best on a test of which of Sternberg's types of intelligence?

Answer: (B) contextual intelligence   Page: 214

16.   Phillip is an eight-year old with a mental age of six. According to Stern's formula, his IQ would be:

Answer: (B) 75.   Page: 216

17.   When you take a test and afterward believe it did not accurately measure your knowledge of the material covered, you are questioning the test's:

Answer: (A) validity.   Page: 217

18.   Dynamic assessment:

Answer: (C) provides a means to minimize cultural bias.   Page: 222

19.   Early interventions designed to enrich the environment of poor children:

Answer: (B) have demonstrated that such efforts can have lasting effects.   Pages: 220-221

20.   When you figure out a solution to your problem and you put it into action, you are engaging in the process of:

Answer: (D) translation.   Page: 226

21.   You are more likely to learn a formal concept from a textbook as opposed to a natural concept.

Answer: True   Pages: 201-202

22.   Framing, or presenting information a certain way to emphasize an outcome or gain, has a limited effect on decision-making.

Answer: False   Page: 204

23.   Anything the human brain can do, an artificial intelligence program can do just as well or better.

Answer: False   Page: 207

24.   Morphemes, the smallest units of meaning in the English language, are always words.

Answer: False   Page: 208

25.   Bilingualism during childhood is associated with an improved ability to think about language.

Answer: True   Page: 211

26.   The SAT is an aptitude tests designed to predict college performance.

Answer: True   Page: 217

27.   Mental retardation is based only on one's IQ score.

Answer: False   Page: 219

28.   Lewis Terman's study found that mentally gifted individuals had more mental health problems than the general population.

Answer: False   Page: 218

29.   Research shows that racial differences in IQ are due to genetic factors.

Answer: False   Pages: 222-223

30.   Women tend to do better than men on mathematical calculation tests.

Answer: True   Pages: 224-225

31.   Discuss the advantages and disadvantages of relying of heuristics in making decisions.

Answer: Heuristics are rules of thumb that are derived from experience and used in decision-making and problem solving. There is no guarantee that a heuristic will be accurate or useful. In general, heuristics enable us to make quick decisions with little mental effort. However, on some of these occasions, more effort would result in more accurate decision-making. Moreover, knowledge about heuristics by advertisers, politicians, and salespeople can lead us to make decisions we might not otherwise have made.   Page: 203

32.   What have attempts to teach language to nonhuman primates demonstrated?

Answer: While virtually all animal species have some form of communication, language appears to be a uniquely human ability. Other primates can be taught to use some components of human language, but they do not appear capable of learning and using the language laws that humans readily internalize. Nonhuman primates are not capable of human speech, so studies have focused on the use of sign language and other symbols for communication. The most impressive results have been obtained with Kanzi, the offspring of a pygmy chimpanzee that had been taught to use symbols for communication. Kanzi has demonstrated an ability to respond to novel commands and has been more prolific than most primates trained to communicate. But despite his success, Kanzi's language abilities are far from what is achieved by human children with little effort.   Pages: 208-210

33.   Distinguish between Spearman's g-factor approach to intelligence and Gardner's theory of multiple intelligences.

Answer: Spearman's g-factor of intelligence suggests that intelligence consists of a single factor, which represents a general intellectual ability that underlies all mental operations. Spearman believed that intelligence tests tap this general factor, as well as several specific factors representing more specific intellectual abilities. In stark contrast, Gardner denies the existence of a general factor, instead suggesting that there are eight independent forms of intelligence, which he labeled frames of mind. The eight frames of mind are: linguistic, logical-mathematical, spatial, bodily-kinesthetic, musical, interpersonal, intrapersonal, and naturalistic. The controversial aspect of Gardner's theory is his assertion that all forms of intelligence are of equal importance.   Pages: 213-214

1. Which of the following is *not* typically considered an act of cognition?

Answer: (D) moving toward an object   Page: 201

2. Although you may think of a tomato as a vegetable, it is actually a fruit. When you categorize a tomato as a fruit, you are using:

Answer: (A) a formal concept.   Page: 201

3. Which pairing best demonstrates a concept and a prototype of that concept?

Answer: (D) furniture - sofa   Page: 202

4. You take multiple choice tests by reading each possible answer and crossing out each one that does not fit, before choosing the one remaining. Which strategy are you using?

Answer: (B) elimination by aspects   Page: 203

5. You see a new story about a plane crash and decide to cancel your trip to Hawaii because you decide that plane crashes have a high likelihood of occurrence. You are relying on the:

Answer: (C) availability heuristic.   Page: 203

6. A thinking strategy based on how closely a new object or situation is judged to resemble an existing prototype is a:

Answer: (B) representativeness heuristic.   Page: 203

7. Corinne's computer sometimes "freezes" when she is surfing the web. Once, she smacked the monitor and the problem was corrected. Since then, the first thing she tries when it freezes is to smack the monitor. She is using the:

Answer: (D) analogy heuristic.   Page: 205

8. "The glass can be half empty or half full." This sentence best illustrates:

Answer: (A) framing.   Page: 204

9. Will solves mazes in his leisure time. When he is doing a maze and reaches a difficult decision on a path to take, he will often look at the end of the maze and try to follow the path until he reaches his position. Will is using the strategy of:

Answer: (B) working backwards.   Page: 205

10.   Using a screwdriver to hammer in a nail demonstrates the ability to rise above:

Answer: (C) functional fixedness.   Page: 206

11.   Which of the following is *not* a morpheme?

Answer: (C) -ive   Page: 208

12.   The meaning or study of meaning of words is called:

Answer: (B) semantics.   Page: 208

13.   According to the linguistic relativity hypothesis:

Answer: (C) because most cultures have just one word for snow, they think about snow in a more limited way than do the Eskimos.   Page: 210

14.   Who is most associated with the idea that there is one general factor (g-factor) underlying our mental abilities?

Answer: (D) Spearman   Page: 213

15.   According to the triarchic theory of intelligence, if someone does very well in school, they would be considered high in which type of intelligence?

Answer: (A) componential intelligence   Page: 214

16.   Carol takes the same intelligence test two years in a row, and her scores both times are the same. Based on this information, this test would be considered to have good:

Answer: (B) reliability.   Page: 216

17.   On the Wechsler scale, the average range of I.Q. is considered to be between:

Answer: (C) 90 and 110.   Page: 218

18.   Which of the following best defines the nature vs. nurture argument in intelligence research?

Answer: (A) How much of intelligence is inherited and how much is due to environmental factors?   Page: 219

19.   Which of the following is the BEST definition of creativity?

Answer: (B) the ability to produce original, valuable ideas or solutions to problems.
        Page: 225

20.   What some people call insight, that sudden awareness of a solution to a problem, is:

Answer: (C) illumination.   Page: 226

21.   Formal concepts are also known as fuzzy concepts.

Answer: False   Pages: 201-202

22.   When an object is visualized, the areas of the brain involved with processing visual information show an increase in activity.

Answer: True   Page: 201

23.   People only rely on intuition to make less important decisions.

Answer: False   Page: 205

24.   Heuristics in general can lead to quick decisions but also leave us open to making errors.

Answer: True   Pages: 203-204

25.   The language learning of both humans and chimps is dependent on operant conditioning.

Answer: False   Pages: 209-210

26.   Learning a second language early in life actually leads to a change in the activity level in Broca's area.

Answer: True   Page: 212

27.   Stern's formula for the calculation of IQ is no longer used today.

Answer: True   Page: 216

28.   Women tend to outperform men on measures of perceptual speed.

Answer: True   Page: 224

29.   Tasks requiring creativity and tasks on intelligence tests rely on different methods of problem-solving.

Answer: True   Page: 226

30.   There are no established tests of creativity.

Answer: False   Pages: 226-227

31.   Describe the limitations of artificial intelligence.

Answer: Computers utilizing artificial intelligence programs can process information at an exceptionally high rate, and perform problem-solving algorithms in a matter of seconds. Programs specifically designed to mimic human functions are called artificial neural networks, but even these programs do now process information exactly the way humans do. Many cognitive tasks performed easily by humans are difficult for computers, such as responding to vague, abstract cues.   Page: 207

32.   What did Lewis Terman find in his study of the mentally gifted?

Answer: Lewis Terman conducted a longitudinal study of gifted students with an average IQ score of 151. His findings countered several stereotypes about gifted people, including the myth that such individuals are physically inferior, Terman's participants exhibited excellent physical, moral, emotional, moral, and social abilities. They also demonstrated better mental health than the general population, earned more academic degrees, achieved higher occupational status, and higher salaries, were better adjusted, and physically healthier.   Page: 218

33.   You are debating Arthur Jensen, Richard Herrnstein, and Charles Murray. How would you answer their arguments regarding race and intelligence?

Answer: In 1969, Jensen published an article in which he attributed the IQ gap between Blacks and Whites to genetic differences between the races, and suggested that environment factors were not likely to significantly alter this difference. In the mid-1990s, Herrnstein and Murray published *The Bell Curve*, in which they argued that 60% of IQ is genetically inherited, and that low IQ is largely immune to change by environmental intervention. However, several studies suggest that race differences are more likely to be the result of poverty and lack of access to educational opportunities than of genetics. The use of dynamic assessment, in which examinees are taught the goal and format of each IQ subtest before actually being tested, increases the number of minority children who achieve above-average IQ scores.   Pages:

1.   The idea that development occurs in distinctive phases that are easily distinguishable from each other is the central premise of:

Answer: (B) stage theories.   Page: 236

2.   Wendy is 18 months old and just learning to speak. She meows whenever she sees a cat. One day, watching television, a rabbit is shown, and Wendy points and meows. What process has Wendy attempted regarding her existing scheme of cats?

Answer: (A) assimilation   Page: 236

3.   Sanford enjoys playing hide-and-seek with his mother. Sanford can play this game only because he has achieved what Piaget would call:

Answer: (D) object permanence.   Page: 237

4.   Piaget's cognitive stages in chronological order are:

Answer: (D) sensorimotor, preoperations, concrete operations, formal operations.   Page: 237

5.   During which of Piaget's stages are children able to understand abstract concepts like "freedom"?

Answer: (A) formal operations   Page: 237

6.   Luis behaves well at school because he wants to please his teacher. Which of Kohlberg's levels of moral development best fits Luis?

Answer: (C) conventional   Page: 242

7.   According the Erikson, adolescence is known as the period of:

Answer: (C) identity vs. role confusion.   Page: 246

8.   Ginny is 82 years old. She often looks back on her life with satisfaction, believing that she accomplished a lot, had a loving family, and contributed to the world. Which of Erikson's stages best fits Ginny?

Answer: (B) ego integrity vs. despair   Page: 246

9.   The developing human organism as it develops from the 9th week until birth is called:

) a fetus.   Page: 247

10.   Because of the risk of Fetal Alcohol Syndrome, pregnant women are advised to:

Answer: (C) completely abstain from alcohol during pregnancy.   Pages: 248-249

11.   Harmful agents in the environment that can have a negative impact on prenatal development are called:

Answer: (B) teratogens.   Page: 248

12.   Brandi is two months old. She is generally happy most of the time, enjoys meeting new people, and has a regular routine to her day. Which temperament best describes her?

Answer: (C) easy   Page: 251

13.   Shawn is 18 months old. Lately, whenever his mother leaves him with his grandmother, he cries as if he is afraid. Their pediatrician said not to worry because _____ is common among children his age.

Answer: (B) separation anxiety   Page: 252

14.   "Mama give cookie me" could be an example of:

Answer: (D) telegraphic speech.   Page:254

15.   Barry tells his father that he and his mother "goed to the store." This error is an example of:

Answer: (B) overregularization.   Page: 254

16.   Which parenting style appears to produce the best results in the United States?

Answer: (A) authoritative   Page: 256

17.   Cassandra is a teenager who hates school. She has developed a plan to have a perfect life that involves quitting school with her boy friend and getting rich and famous by being on "American Idol." Cassandra's plan would best be described by which term?

Answer: (B) naïve idealism   Page: 238

18.   The most common symptom of menopause is:

Answer: (B) hot flashes.   Page: 260

19.   The only intellectual ability to show a continuous decline from age 30 to 80 is:

Answer: (B) perceptual speed.   Page: 261

20.   The three leading causes of death in both men and women over age 65 are heart disease, cancer and:

Answer: (B) stroke.   Page: 263

21.   Developmental psychology as it is studied today focuses on childhood and adolescence as times of change, and adulthood as a time of stagnation.

Answer: False   Page: 235

22.   According to Piaget, a 3-year-old child would assume that you can see what she sees.

Answer: True   Page: 237

23.   Vygotsky's sociocultural approach to cognitive development puts more emphasis on the impact of language development than does Piaget's theory.

Answer: True   Page: 241

24.   Newborns can recognize stimuli to which they were exposed prior to birth.

Answer: True   Page: 247

25.   One conclusion drawn from the visual cliff experiment was that babies have no perception of depth until they learn to walk.

Answer: False   Page: 250

26.   Securely attached infants tend to develop more advanced social skills when they are preschoolers than peers who were not securely attached.

Answer: True   Page: 253

27.   The nativist position suggests that language development occurs primarily through operant conditioning.

Answer: False   Page: 255

28.   Gender roles occur through the sole influence of biological factors.

Answer: False   Page: 257

29.   Fluid intelligence peaks in one's 20s, but crystallized intelligence increases throughout the life span.

Answer: True   Page: 263

30.   White males over 75 have the highest suicide rate of any group in the United States.

Answer: True   Page: 265

31.   Name and describe four types of conservation tasks used by Piaget.

Answer: Conservation is the concept that a given quantity of matter remains the same despite being rearranged or changed in appearance, as long as nothing is added or taken away. Piaget believed that conservation develops during the concrete operations stage, from ages 7-11 or 12. Different conservation concepts occur at different times, and in a certain sequence. Conservation of number develops between 6-7 years of age. In the original presentation, two equal lines of coins are shown to the child. In the transformation, one row is condensed closer together, and the child must recognize that the two rows still contain the same number of coins. Conservation of liquid develops between 6-7 years of age. In the original presentation, two equally filled glasses of juice are shown to the child. In the transformation, one glass of juice is emptied into a taller, thinner glass, and the child must recognize that the two glasses still contain the same amount of juice. Conservation of mass develops between 6-7 years of age. In the original presentation, two equal balls of clay are shown to the child. In the transformation, one ball of clay is smashed into a flat pancake, and the child must recognize that the ball and pancake still contain the same amount of clay. Finally, conservation of area develops between 8-10 years of age. In the original presentation, two pictures of a cow with an equal field of grass are shown to the child. In the transformation, one picture is exchanged for another with the same cow, but the field of grass has been strewn throughout the picture, rather than in one discrete region, and the child must recognize that the two images still contain the same amount of grass.   Page: 239

32.   Distinguish between how learning theorists and nativists explain language development.

Answer: Nativists argue that humans are born prepared to acquire language. A famous linguist, Noam Chomsky, has even argued that humans are born with a language acquisition device (LAD), which enables children to extract the rules of their native language from what they hear. While the LAD has not been located, an examination of the universal commonalities in language learning supports the notion of an inborn ability to decipher the rules of language. Further evidence of a role for nature in language learning is found in the manner in which language is acquired, because all children pass through the same identifiable stages in learning language. Learning theorists argue that language is learned through reinforcement and imitation. While certainly children appear to acquire aspects of language through these processes, this theory is inconsistent with the errors observed because they are errors that a child is unlikely to have ever heard or been rewarded for.   Pages: 254-255

33.   Describe how social learning, cognitive-developmental, and gender schema theorists explain gender role development.

Answer: Gender roles are cultural expectations about the behavior appropriate for each gender. Social learning theorists suggest that environmental influences best explain gender role development. Specifically, they suggest that children are reinforced for imitating behaviors that are gender-role appropriate, and reprimanded when engaging in gender-role-inappropriate behaviors. Cognitive-developmental theorists such as Kohlberg suggest that an understanding of gender is a prerequisite to gender role development. According to Kohlberg's theory, children go through a series of stages in acquiring the concept of gender. First they acquire a gender identity, an understanding that they are male or female. Then, children acquire the concept of gender stability, the awareness that their gender does not change. Finally, children acquire the concept of gender constancy, that regardless of what they do or wear, they remain that same gender. In addition, Kohlberg states that children are motivated to seek out same-sex models and top act in ways that are gender role-appropriate. Gender-schema theorists like Sandra Bem, suggests that younger children are motivated to behave in ways consistent with gender-based standards and stereotypes. But Bem suggests that this process occurs when gender identity is formed, rather than later, as cognitive-developmentalists suggest. Moreover, Bem suggests that a child's self-esteem increases their motivation to align behavior with culturally defined gender roles.
Pages: 257-258

1.   Which of the following did *not* propose a stage theory of development?

Answer: (a) Ainsworth   Page: 253

2.   An infant can be said to possess a scheme for nursing at his or her mother's breast. When the infant has to modify this scheme to nurse from a bottle, which process can be said to occur?

Answer: (A) accommodation   Page: 236

3.   Shayna wants two cookies, but her mother wants her to only have one. So her mother breaks one in half, and Shayna happily believes she has two. Shayna has not yet developed the concept of:

Answer: (C) conservation.   Page: 237

4.   Chris pretends that playing cards are actually people interacting with one another. Piaget would say that Chris is using:

Answer: (C) symbolic function.   Page: 237

5.   Kohlberg believed that moral development is closely related to:

Answer: (C) cognitive development.   Page: 241

6.   Quentin behaves well so that he can avoid getting spanked by his parents. Kohlberg would say that he is at which level of moral development?

Answer: (A) preconventional   Page: 242

7.   Erikson's first stage, the outcome of which depends on how responsive a child's caregiver is to that child's needs, is called:

Answer: (C) basic trust vs. mistrust.   Page: 245

8.   The cell that results from the union of a sperm and egg, corresponding to the first two weeks of pregnancy, is called the:

Answer: (B) zygote.   Page: 247

9.   During which prenatal period do the major organs of the body develop?

Answer: (A) period of the embryo   Page: 247

10.   Which of the following statements about neonates is *false*?

Answer: (C) Newborns are blind at birth, and develop sight starting around 5 weeks of age.
        Page: 249

11.   Temperament:

Answer: (B) appears to be correlated with personality later in life.   Page: 251

12.   Karen clings tightly to her mother in virtually all situations. She will not explore new environments. If her mother leaves the room for a few minutes, Karen will be angry at her mother and not allow her mother to hold her. Which type of attachment is Karen demonstrating?

Answer: (C) resistant   Page: 253

13.   The phoneme vocalization that occurs usually between 4 – 6 months is called:

Answer: (B) babbling.   Page: 254

14.   Seeing her father in a kilt, Sally exclaimed "Daddy is a girl! He's wearing a skirt!" With this statement, Sally is exhibiting that she has not yet acquired the concept of:

Answer: (D) gender constancy.   Page: 257

15.   Which approach suggests that children learn gender roles primarily by being rewarded for behaviors that are considered gender-appropriate?

Answer: (C) social learning theory   Page: 257

16.   Sixteen-year-old Carlos loves action movies. Whenever he sees a new action film, he likes to try to copy the kinds of stunts he sees on the screen. He is convinced he can never be seriously hurt doing this, because of:

Answer: (A) the personal fable.   Page: 238

17.   Presbyopia is considered an unavoidable change that occurs:

Answer: (B) around the mid to late forties.   Page: 260

18.   Relationship satisfaction tends to decline in adults following the birth of a child. Research has shown this decline to be primarily due to conflicts over:

Answer: (D) the division of labor in raising a child.   Page: 261

19.   Which type of intelligence peaks in the early 20s and slowly declines thereafter?

Answer: (B) fluid   Page: 263

20.   Which of the following is not a physical change typically associated with aging?

Answer: (A) becoming more nearsighted   Pages: 262-263

21.   It is generally agreed that cognitive development occurs in discrete stages.

Answer: False   Page: 236

22.   Vygotsky's "zone of proximal development" refers to those tasks a child has mastered.

Answer: False   Page: 241

23.   Erikson's stage theory is unique in its emphasis on development throughout the life span.

Answer: True   Page: 245

24.   Characteristics of children with fetal alcohol syndrome include mental retardation and hyperactivity.

Answer: True   Pages: 248-249

25.   If a child does not meet a developmental milestone for a motor skill within two months later than the average child, then that child is considered unhealthy.

Answer: False   Page: 250

26.   On average, girls undergo the adolescent growth spurt earlier than boys.

Answer: True   Page: 258

27.   Adolescents tend to choose friends who have a similar background and values.

Answer: True   Page: 260

28.   About 80% of women with school-aged children work outside the home.

Answer: True   Page: 261

29.   Physical exercise has little impact on the health of older adults.

Answer: False   Page: 263

30.   Over 75% of all cases of senility are the result of Alzheimer's disease.

Answer: False   Page: 264

31.   Describe each of Piaget's stages of cognitive development, being sure to also describe the abilities and limitations at each stage.

Answer: Piaget's initial stage of cognitive development is the sensorimotor stage (age birth to two years), in which infants develop object permanence, the realization that objects continue to exist even when they are out of sight. At this stage children are still limited to primarily reflexive thought. The second stage is the preoperational stage (ages 2-7 years), during which children acquire the symbolic function, the understanding that one thing can symbolize another. Children begin to engage in pretend play at this stage. The limitation at this stage is egocentrism, as children are unable to realize that others cannot see what they see, hear what they hear, and think what they think. The third stage is the concrete operations stage (ages 7-11 or 12 years), marked by the development of conservation, the concept that a given quantity of matter remains the same despite being rearranged or changed in appearance, as long as nothing is added or taken away. The limitation at this stage is that children still think concretely, and cannot apply logic to hypothetical situations. The fourth stage is formal operations (age 11 or 12 and beyond), in which children develop the ability to base logical reasoning on a hypothetical premise, or hypothetico-deductive reasoning.   Pages: 237-238

32.   Describe the three parenting styles. Which produces the best results?

Answer: Studies by Diane Baumrind have identified three parenting styles that differ based on the level of control and communication that occurs. Authoritarian parents are strict and controlling. The authoritarian parent expects to be obeyed and does not tolerate being questioned. The authoritative parent sets limits, but is communicative. The authoritative parent expects obedience, but will discuss the reasoning that underlies the demands made or the punishment delivered. Permissive parents establish few rules, if any, and exert little or no control. In the United States, authoritative parenting is associated with children who are mature, responsible, and socially competent. There are, however, exceptions to this. Children raised in a traditional Asian culture may benefit more from authoritarian parenting. It is thought that this may occur because the children believe their parents require obedience because they love them. Page: 256

33.   What effects does the timing of puberty have on males and females?

Answer: Puberty is a period of rapid physical growth and change that culminates in sexual maturity. The average onset for puberty is age 10 for girls, and age 12 for boys, although there is a wide range for that onset among normally developing adolescents. Early-maturing boys tend to be taller and more athletic than their peers, and this have a positive body image, to feel confident, secure, independent, and happy, as well as to have greater academic success. However, they may be more hostile and aggressive than later-maturing peers. Early-maturing girls feel self-conscious about their developing bodies and their size, and are thus more likely to develop eating disorders than later-developing girls. They also tend to have earlier sexual experiences, more unwanted pregnancies, and are more likely to be exposed to alcohol and drug use. Late-maturing girls often experience stress over failing to develop physically along with their peers, but tend to be slimmer and taller.
Pages: 258-259

1.   Keisha wants to make good grades because her parents promised her a new car if she makes the honor roll. Keisha's motivation is:

Answer: (B) extrinsic.   Page: 278

2.   Human behavior is motivated by certain innate tendencies shared by all individuals, according to:

Answer: (A) instinct theory.   Page: 279

3.   Which of the following statements is *true* according to the Yerkes-Dodson law?

Answer: (D) Performance on difficult tasks is better when arousal is low.   Page: 280

4.   Which needs did Maslow believe must be satisfied first?

Answer: (A) physiological   Page: 281

5.   Which of the following factors *inhibits* eating?

Answer: (C) increased levels of cholecystokinin (CCK)   Page: 283

6.   Which of the following is a primary drive?

Answer: (C) thirst   Page: 283

7.   You conduct a hunger experiment with rats. In one rat, you damage the ventromedial hypothalamus. In the second rat, you stimulate the lateral hypothalamus. Then you offer food to each of them. What will happen?

Answer: (C) Both rats will eat.   Page: 283

8.   Cherelle has been at around 120 pounds for most of her adult life. She doesn't work hard to lose weight, nor does she try to gain weight. You conclude that 120 pounds represents Cherelle's:

Answer: (A) set point.   Page: 285

9.   The hormone that directly affects the hypothalamus and plays a primary role in weight regulation is:

Answer: (B) leptin.   Page: 284

10.   What one factor seems to correlate with male bulimics?

Answer: (C) sexual orientation   Page: 287

11.   What is the shortest of the four phases in the sexual response cycle?

Answer: (D) orgasm   Page: 296

12.   The area of the hypothalamus that governs sexual behavior is twice as large in heterosexual men than it is in homosexual men, according to research done by LeVay. What is the main criticism of LeVay's research?

Answer: (B) AIDS was a variable that was not accounted for.   Page: 298

13.   Inez devotes all of her energy to school. She sets high standards of performance for herself in an effort to accomplish all she can. Inez could be said to have a high:

Answer: (C) need for achievement.   Page: 282

14.   Yvonne insists she must get the highest grade on every test so that she can exceed her peers and enhance her own self-worth. According to goal orientation theory, which goal orientation best fits Yvonne?

Answer: (C) performance-approach orientation   Pages: 282-283

15.   On realizing that the shadow behind you is a man with a gun, your heart begins to race and at the same time you feel afraid. With which of the following theories of emotion is this scenario most consistent?

Answer: (A) Cannon-Bard Theory   Page: 288

16.   Which theory of emotion says that emotion-provoking stimuli trigger a cognitive appraisal, followed by emotional and physiological arousal?

Answer: (D) Lazarus Theory   Page: 288

17.   Which of the following would *not* be considered a basic emotion?

Answer: (A) embarassment   Page: 290

18.   Many in traditional British culture consider Americans to be vulgar because of the Americans' tendency to spontaneously demonstrate whatever emotion they feel. The conflict between cultures is caused by differing:

Answer: (B) display rules.   Page: 290

19.   The facial feedback hypothesis states:

Answer: (C) that muscular movements involved in certain facial expressions produce the corresponding emotion.   Page: 291

20.   Which of the following has been suggested as providing a biological explanation accounting for some of the emotional differences between the genders?

Answer: (A) Women process emotions in both cerebral hemispheres, while men tend to use predominantly the left hemisphere to process emotions.   Page: 292

21.   A motive can be biological or social in nature, but no behavior serves both types of motives at once.

Answer: False   Page: 277

22.   Extrinsic motivation is consistent with Skinner's concept of reinforcement.

Answer: True   Page: 278

23.   The phenomenon of sensation-seeking is best explained by drive-reduction theory.

Answer: False   Page: 279

24.   Individuals with bulimia nervosa are often of normal weight.

Answer: True   Page: 286

25.   Women appear to have the strongest desire for sex around the time of ovulation when they are most likely to conceive a child, as evolutionary theory would predict.

Answer: True   Page: 294

26.   Androgens are only present in men; estrogen and progesterone are only present in women.

Answer: False   Page: 297

27.   Younger siblings show a higher need for achievement than older siblings.

Answer: False   Page: 282

28.   The amygdala is activated by fear before any direct involvement of the cerebral cortex occurs.

Answer: True   Page: 289

29.   Blind babies develop facial expressions of emotions in the same sequence and at the same time as infants who can see.

Answer: True   Page: 290

30.   Women report more intense emotional experience than men, but men generate more extreme physiological reactions indicating emotional response.

Answer: False   Page: 293

31.   Describe environmental cues for hunger.

Answer: Hunger is influenced by both physiological processes and environmental factors. Environmental cues that stimulate eating include an appetizing smell, taste, or appearance of food, acquired food preferences, being around others who are eating, foods high in fat and sugar, learned eating habits, and eating as a reaction to boredom, stress, or an unpleasant emotional state. Environmental cues that inhibit eating include an unappetizing smell, taste, or appearance of food, acquired taste aversions, learned eating habits, a desire to be thin, and not eating as a reaction to boredom, stress, or an unpleasant emotional state.   Pages: 283-284

32.   Define anorexia nervosa and bulimia nervosa and describe the negative effects of each disorder.

Answer: Anorexia nervosa and bulimia nervosa are both eating disorders. Anorexia nervosa is characterized by an overwhelming, irrational fear of gaining weight or becoming fat, compulsive dieting to the point of self-starvation, and excessive weight loss. Anorexics have a grossly distorted perception of their body size. Anorexics also attempt to lose weight through relentless exercise. Negative effects of anorexia nervosa include amenorrhea, low blood pressure, impaired heart function, dehydration, electrolyte disturbances, and sterility. Bulimia nervosa is characterized by repeated and uncontrolled episodes of binge eating, which involves the consumption of large amounts of food and a feeling of being unable to control eating behavior during a binge. Bulimics may follow binges with purges, attempts to maintain their weight with self-induced vomiting or the use of laxatives. Negative effects of bulimia nervosa include tooth decay due to the presence of stomach acids during vomiting, chronic sore throat, dehydration, swelling of the salivary glands, kidney damage, and hair loss. Depression, guilt, and shame are common feelings among bulimics as well.   Pages: 285-286

33.   Discuss the role of cognition in each of the four theories of emotion discussed in this chapter.

Answer: The role of cognition, the influence of thinking, in emotion has long been a subject of debate. Do we respond automatically to a snake with fear, or do we consider first whether or not it is poisonous? Interestingly, the two earliest theories of emotion virtually ignored the role of cognition in emotion. Neither the James-Lange nor the Cannon-Bard theory addressed the role of cognition in emotion. Each of these theories envisioned an emotional response as an automatic response to a stimulus. A very different approach was introduced by Schachter and Singer. These researchers cited cognition as a key element in determining what emotion would be experienced. According to the Schachter-Singer theory, an emotion is felt after two things have occurred: physiological arousal and a labeling of that arousal. In other words, arousal is felt and then this arousal is interpreted according to the situation. A very different view is offered by Lazarus. While James-Lange and Cannon-Bard ignored cognition and Schacter-Singer saw it as following arousal, Lazarus proposed that the first step in an emotional response is cognitive. According to Lazarus, an emotion is not felt until the situation has been subjected to a cognitive appraisal. No theory is without its flaws, but all invite a more careful consideration of the processes involved in the experience of an emotion.   Pages: 287-288

1.   Gerrard just got a promotion at work. He told his family that he didn't really care about the extra money – he was thrilled because he liked his work and took pride in doing a good job. Gerrard's motivation is:

Answer: (a) intrinsic.   Page: 278

2.   According to drive-reduction theory, a drive is created when the body's balanced internal state is disturbed. This balanced state is called:

Answer: (C) homeostasis.   Page: 279

3.   Which of the following is not consistent with Maslow's hierarchy of needs?

Answer: (B) A woman deprives herself of food to lose weight and gain approval from her friends.   Page: 281

4.   Removal of which brain area will lead to an animal's eating itself to obesity?

Answer: (C) the ventromedial hypothalamus   Page: 283

5.   Which of the following environmental factors inhibits eating?

Answer: (D) none of the above inhibits eating   Page: 284

6.   As you get older, you find you cannot eat the same quantity and types of foods you ate when you were younger without putting on extra weight. This is due to a change in your:

Answer: (A) metabolic rate.   Page: 285

7.   Grace is obsessed with her body. She thinks she is fat when she is actually alarmingly thin. She counts every calorie and no matter what the scale says, she is convinced that she is grossly overweight. Grace probably suffers from _____.

Answer: (B) anorexia nervosa.   Page: 285

8.   Gender differences are seen in all of the following *except*:

Answer: (B) the role of hormones in sexual interest.   Page: 293

9.   Which of the following is *true* according to the evolutionary principle of parental investment?

Answer: (D) Women seek older men who are stable and emotionally attached.   Page: 294

10.   What do men experience during the resolution phase?

Answer: (C) refractory period   Page: 297

11.   In Laumann's survey, what percentage of men reported having felt some same-sex desires?

Answer: (C) 10%   Page: 298

12.   Which of the following has not been suggested as a way to encourage the development of high need for achievement in children?

Answer: (A) giving children fewer responsibilities so they can concentrate on schoolwork
        Page: 282

13.   What is the name of the test used to reveal a person's needs and the strength of them?

Answer: (A) Thematic Apperception Test   Page: 282

14.   Adam studies enough in school to make sure he manages to score at least as high as the class average on every exam. According to goal orientation theory, which goal orientation best fits Adam?

Answer: (D) performance-avoidance orientation   Page:282

15.   After falling, a child often looks toward the mother before reacting. Depending on how the mother responds, the child will respond to the fall by either laughing or crying. Which of the following would best explain this phenomenon?

Answer: (C) Schacter-Singer theory   Page: 288

16.   Which theory suggests that emotion-provoking stimuli is transmitted to the brain and nervous system simultaneously, causing both physiological and emotional responses?

Answer: (B) Cannon-Bard Theory   Page: 288

17.   Which of the following are both universal and unlearned?

Answer: (D) Basic emotions   Page: 290

18.   Which of the following statements is *true* concerning brain lateralization and emotions?

Answer: (A) Sad feelings are associated with greater activity in the left side of the brain.
Page: 289

19.   Which of the following is an example of a display rule?

Answer: (D) Girls will smile when presented with a gift, even if they do not like it.   Page: 290

20.   Your psychology professor suggested that you hold a pencil between your teeth. As your mouth curved into a smile you began to feel happy. Your professor was demonstrating

_____.

Answer: (B) facial feedback hypothesis.   Page: 291

21.   Intrinsically motivated behaviors are typically considered more enjoyable than extrinsically motivated behaviors.

Answer: True   Page: 278

22.   Humans have several instincts that serve to motivate behavior.

Answer: False   Page: 279

23.   Low-carbohydrate diets may reduce one's metabolic rate, which in turn drains the dieter's energy so that they are less able to exercise.

Answer: True   Page: 285

24.   No matter what treatment program is used, most individuals with anorexia nervosa experience relapses.

Answer: True   Page: 286

25.   There is ample evidence for some kind of genetic predisposition that increases the likelihood of homosexuality in men, but not in women.

Answer: False   Pages: 298-299

26.   Men are more likely to have sexual fantasies of doing something sexual to someone else, whereas women are more likely to have sexual fantasies of having something sexual done to them.

Answer: True   Page: 297

27.   Individuals with a high need for achievement choose easier tasks on which th certain to have success.

Answer: False   Page: 282

28.   College and high school students who adopt one of the mastery orientations are more likely to procrastinate and get poorer grades.

Answer: False   Page: 283

29.   Research has indicated that it is always healthy to express one's emotions.

Answer: False   Page: 291

30.   Women appear to be more physiologically sensitive to negative emotions than men are.

Answer: True   Page: 292

31.   Compare and contrast the drive reduction theory and the arousal theory of motivation.

Answer: Drive-reduction theory proposes that motives (drives) are created when needs are not met. More specifically, when homeostasis is not maintained, a need arises and we are motivated to restore equilibrium. While drive-reduction theory explains the drive to fill most biological needs, it does not explain the behavior of those who seek to disrupt homeostasis, as in the case of those who seek thrills (as opposed to merely striving to avoid boredom). Arousal theory does explain the behavior of thrill seekers and proposes that we all strive to achieve some optimal level of arousal (alertness). When our state is other than that desired level, we seek some excitement or strive to reduce the level of stimulation that we are experiencing. A significant difference between the two theories is that drive reduction theory suggests our motivations occur to erase an aversive state (a drive), whereas arousal theory suggests our motivations occur to strive to achieve a desirable state (optimal arousal).   Pages: 279-280

32.   Describe the phases of the human sexual response cycle, highlighting the main differences between men and women throughout the cycle.

Answer: Masters and Johnson concluded that both men and women experience a sexual response cycle containing four phases. First is the excitement stage, during which external cues initiate the sexual response. Visual cues are more likely to initiate this phase in men than in women, whereas women respond more to loving touches and verbal expressions of love. In both partners, muscular tension increases, heart rate quickens, and blood pressure rises. The man's penis becomes erect, and the woman's clitoris swells. Vaginal lubrication also increases. During the plateau phase, blood pressure and muscle tension increase, and breathing becomes heavy and more rapid. The man's testes swell, and the woman's vagina swells. The clitoris withdraws under the clitoral hood. The orgasm phase is marked by a sudden discharge of accumulated sexual pleasure. Orgasm is marked by body-wide muscular contractions. Men first perceive the inevitability of ejaculation, and then the ejaculation of semen from the penis occurs in forceful spurts. The female orgasm typically lasts longer than the male's. Finally, during the resolution phase, the body returns to its unaroused state. Men experience a refractory period, during which they cannot have another orgasm, which may last from a few minutes to several hours. Women may achieve another orgasm with continued stimulation, as they do not experience a refractory period.   Pages: 296-297

33.   Describe gender differences in the experience and expression of emotions.

Answer: Research indicates that men and women express emotions differently, as well as experiencing differing levels of emotional intensity. For example, women are as likely as men to express anger privately, but are less likely to do so in public. One reason for this might be that in the United States, emotion display rules tend to be gender-specific. Women are expected to suppress negative emotions and express positive ones, while the opposite expectation is made of men. Research has also indicated that, of the five basic emotions of joy, love, fear, sadness, and anger, women report more intense and frequent emotions than did men, with the exception of anger. Physiological measures verified those self-reports.   Page: 292

1.   Which of the following is *not* part of the text's definition of stress?

Answer: (B) an emotional response   Page: 309

2.   Which type of stressors seem to cause more stress?

Answer: (A) hassles   Page: 311

3.   Hank has a stressful job, but he always looks forward to coming home to his wife, who never fails to bring a smile to his face and relieve some of his stress. According to Richard Lazarus, Hank's time with his wife would be described as:

Answer: (D) an uplift.   Page: 311

4.   Would you rather have a terrible toothache, or have the undesirable experience of having the tooth drilled and the cavity filled? This choice represents what type of conflict?

Answer: (C) avoidance-avoidance   Page: 312

5.   According to Albrecht, which of the following factors is *not* related to job satisfaction and effective functioning at work?

Answer: (C) being one's own boss   Page: 313

6.   A prolonged stress reaction following a catastrophic experience is_____.

Answer: (B) Post-Traumatic Stress Disorder.   Page: 314

7.   Which of the following has been found to moderate levels of racial stress in African Americans?

Answer: (A) a strong sense of ethnic identity   Page: 315

8.   According to Seyle's GAS concept, when an organism fails in its efforts to resist a stressor, what happens?

Answer: (B) exhaustion   Page: 316

9.   According to Richard Lazarus, an event appraised as stressful could involve:

Answer: (D) all of the above.   Pages: 316-317

10.   Which of the following is the best example of a secondary appraisal?

Answer: (C) Jan decides that she isn't smart enough to do well in school.   Page: 317

11.   Mrs. Genova has been told that she has terminal cancer and only a few months left to live. After a brief time, she set out to tie up the loose ends of her life, updating her will, giving away special possessions and saying goodbyes. Mrs. Genova is employing which approach to coping with her illness?

Answer: (C) emotion-focused   Page: 317

12.   The biomedical model focuses on _____, giving explanations based on biological factors without taking social or psychological matters into account.

Answer: (D) illness   Page: 318

13.   Which element of the Type A behavior pattern is most related to coronary heart disease?

Answer: (B) hostility   Page: 320

14.   Which of the following is *not* a risk factor for cancer, according to health psychologists?

Answer: (D) all of the above are risk factors for cancer   Page: 321

15.   The key components of the immune system are the white blood cells known as:

Answer: (C) lymphocytes.   Page: 322

16.   Which of the following infectious diseases has *not* been correlated with periods of high stress?

Answer: (A) rubella   Page: 322

17.   Which of the following qualities is *not* considered part of the trait of hardiness?

Answer: (C) caring   Page: 323

18.   What percentage of the adult population in this country still smokes, according to your text?

Answer: (B) less than 25%   Page: 325

19.   Shrinkage to which part of the brain has been shown in MRI studies done on alcoholics?

Answer: (C) cerebral cortex.   Page: 327

20.   A diagnosis of AIDS is made when:

Answer: (D) the damage to the immune system due to HIV leads to opportunistic infections.
        Page: 328

21.   The parasympathetic nervous system initiates the fight-or-flight response.

Answer: False   Page: 309

22.   The hassle most commonly cited by college students was not getting enough sleep.

Answer: False   Page: 311

23.   Survivor guilt is a common symptom of individuals who live through a catastrophic event.

Answer: True   Page: 314

24.   Prolonged stress can lead to permanent increases in blood pressure, suppression of the immune system, and weakening of muscles.

Answer: True   Page: 316

25.   Research has indicated that problem-focused coping is the best stress-management strategy.

Answer: False   Page: 318

26.   A sedentary life style is the primary modifiable risk factor contributing to death from coronary heart disease.

Answer: True   Page: 319

27.   Once a stressful experience has passed, stress no longer actively suppresses the immune system.

Answer: False   Page: 322

28.   Women are more likely than men to seek medical care.

Answer: True   Page: 324

29.   Being exposed to second-hand smoke doubles one's risk of having a heart attack.

Answer: True   Page: 326

30.   The most common infectious disease in the United States is AIDS.

Answer: False   Page: 327

31.   Describe the biopsychosocial model of health and illness.

Answer: The biopsychosocial model considers health and illness to be determined by a combination of biological, psychological, and social factors. Biological factors favoring health and wellness include genetics, homeostasis, relaxation, and a healthy lifestyle. Those biological factors working against health and wellness include lack of exercise, poor diet, disease and injury, toxic chemicals, and pollution. Psychological factors favoring health and wellness include self-regulation, stress management, giving and receiving love, positive imagery, positive thoughts, and a healthy personality. Psychological factors working against health and wellness include depression, negative thoughts, worry, anxiety, poor coping skills, an unhealthy personality, and stress. Social factors favoring health and wellness include social responsibility, social policy, and social groups. Social factors working against health and wellness include loneliness, poverty, exploitation, and violence.   Page: 318-319

32.   Describe the Type A and Type B behavior patterns.

Answer: The Type A behavior pattern is associated with a high rate of coronary heart disease. People with the Type A behavior pattern have a strong sense of time urgency, are impatient, excessively competitive, hostile, and easily angered. People with the Type B behavior pattern are relaxed and easygoing and are not driven by a sense of time urgency. They are not impatient or hostile and are able to relax without guilt.   Page: 320

33.   Describe four personal factors that reduce the impact of stress and illness.

Answer: Four personal factors that reduce the impact of stress and illness are optimism, hardiness, religious involvement, and social support. Optimists generally expect good outcomes, and these positive expectations make them more stress-resistant than pessimists, who generally expect bad outcomes. Hardiness is a combination of three psychological qualities – commitment, control, and change – shared by people who can handle high levels of stress and remain healthy. People with this characteristic tend to act to solve their problems, and to welcome life's challenges, seeing them as opportunities for growth and improvement. Research also indicates that religious involvement is positively associated with measures of physical health and lower rates of cancer, heart disease, and stroke. Finally, social support refers to tangible and/or emotional support provided in times of need by family members, friends, and others; such support provides a feeling of being loved, valued, and cared for by those toward whom we feel a similar obligation.   Pages: 323-324

1.   You are about to ask your boss for a much-needed raise. The physiological response involving the release of hormones that cause you to feel anxious is called:

Answer: (C) the fight-or-flight response.   Page: 309

2.   What is the SRRS?

Answer: (C) Social Readjustment Rating Scale   Page: 309

3.   If you like all kinds of sweets…do you want cake or ice cream? This choice represents what type of conflict?

Answer: (B) approach-approach   Page: 312

4.   What does your book report as the number one hassle for college students?

Answer: (A) worry about the future   Page: 311

5.   Which of the following is *not* typically considered a result of job stress?

Answer: (A) family conflict   Page: 313

6.   Posttraumatic stress disorder (PTSD):

Answer: (D) is often associated with the development of other psychological problems.
          Page: 314

7.   Historical racism has been associated with:

Answer: (C) cardiovascular reactivity.   Page: 315

8.   Cara works two jobs while trying to support her two children and take care of her elderly father. She initially struggled with this arrangement, but more recently she feels as though she is handling the stress better. Which stage of the general adaptation syndrome seems to best fit Cara?

Answer: (A) the resistance stage.   Page: 316

9.   Mr. Stanley has cancer. He spends all of his spare time reading and doing research into alternative medicine and experimental treatments for his disease. He is determined to beat it. Mr. Stanley is using which approach to coping with his illness?

Answer: (B) problem-focused   Page: 317

10.   Dr. Laslow is conducting a biopsychosocial evaluation of a patient. He has evaluated the patient's mood, stress management skills, level of exercise, diet, and personality. What has Dr. Laslow forgotten?

Answer: (C) He has not assessed social factors.   Page: 318

11.   Which of the following statements about the Type B behavior pattern is *false*?

Answer: (D) Type B individuals are less ambitious than Type A individuals.   Page: 320

12.   The field that includes psychologists, biologists, and medical researchers who study the effects of psychological factors on the immune system is called:

Answer: (A) psychoneuroimmunology   Page: 322

13.   Which of the following has *not* been linked to lowered immune response?

Answer: (C) job responsibilities   Page: 322

14.   Religious faith:

Answer: (B) has been shown to be correlated with better health habits.   Page: 323

15.   Which of the following is *not* a potential benefit of social support?

Answer: (A) reduction of likelihood of development of cancer   Page: 323

16.   Which statement concerning ethnic differences in health conditions is *false*?

Answer: (C) Hispanic Americans suffer more heart problems than non-Hispanic White Americans.   Page: 324

17.   Which of the following is *not* considered a negative consequence of smoking?

Answer: (C) higher incidence of anxiety disorders and depression   Page: 326

18.   The most frequently abused substance of all is likely:

Answer: (A) alcohol.   Page: 326

19.   The incidence of many sexually transmitted diseases (STDs) has increased over the last 30 years because of all of the following *except*:

Answer: (C) increased use of vaginal spermicides.   Page: 327

20. AIDS progresses more quickly in all of the following *except*:

Answer: (A) men.   Page: 329

21. While people vary in what they view as a hassle, those events seen as catastrophes are universal.

Answer: False   Page: 311

22. Unpredictable stressors are more difficult to cope with than predictable stressors.

Answer: True   Page: 312

23. PTSD is a common response to typical life stressors.

Answer: False   Page: 314

24. Racial stress can only be experienced in an environment where racism occurs.

Answer: False   Page: 315

25. Ignoring a stressor can be an effective way of managing stress.

Answer: True   Page: 318

26. Research indicates that the most effective elements for a strategy of coping with cancer are social support, focusing on the positive, and distraction.

Answer: True   Page: 321

27. Having a rich social life may reduce the risk of catching a cold virus.

Answer: True   Page: 322

28. Men are more likely to die following open-heart surgery than women.

Answer: False   Page: 324

29. Ninety percent of ex-smokers report that they quit on their own.

Answer: True   Page: 326

30.   Viral STDs are more treatable than bacterial STDs.

Answer: False   Page: 328

31.   Review the variables that must be within a person's comfort zone to experience job satisfaction, according to Albrecht.

Answer: Albrecht suggests that if people are to function effectively and find satisfaction on the job, the following variables must fall within their comfort zone. Either too much or too little of these factors for a specific individual may compromise their job satisfaction. First, their workload must be balanced to keep them from feeling anxious, frustrated, and unrewarded. The job description and evaluation criteria must be clear to avoid confusion and anxiety. Physical variables such as temperature, noise, humidity, pollution, amount of work space, etc., must fit the person's level of comfort. The job status should suit the individual's needs and ability to handle stress. The accountability load must provide equivalent levels of responsibility and control. The task variety should provide a comfortable level of stimulation. The amount of human contact should suit the individual's preferences and personality. The physical challenge on the job should meet a person's ability to manage. Finally, the mental challenge of the job should meet one's needs and capabilities.   Pages: 312-313

32.   Describe Lazarus and Folkman's psychological model of stress.

Answer: According to Lazarus and Folkman, a person's perception of a stressor causes stress, more so than the stressor itself. When people are confronted with a potentially stressful event, they engage in a process that requires two type of appraisal. First, they engage in a primary appraisal, a cognitive evaluation of a potentially stressful event to determine whether its effect is positive, irrelevant, or negative. When a situation may involve threat, harm, or loss, an individual is likely to experience fear, anger, or resentment. If instead the situation is perceived as a challenge or opportunity, the person typically experiences excitement, hopefulness, and eagerness. Secondary appraisal is a cognitive evaluation of available resources and options prior to deciding how to deal with a stressor. The person judges whether available resources and time are adequate to deal with the stressor. If they are judges sufficient, the person experiences less subjective stress than if the resources are perceived to be inadequate for the situation at hand. Pages: 316-317

33.   Discuss the lifestyle factors that put one at risk for coronary heart disease.

Answer: While there is nothing that we can do about the genes we inherit, how we live our lives can either increase or decrease the likelihood that we will remain healthy. Coronary heart disease has been clearly linked to numerous lifestyle factors. Living a sedentary lifestyle puts people at risk for coronary heart disease. People who engage in less than 20 minutes of exercise three times a week should work to increase their activity level. Other risk factors include high cholesterol levels (usually modifiable with dietary changes), smoking, and high blood pressure. Personality variables that may increase blood pressure have also been found to be associated with coronary heart disease. The so-called Type A personality is characterized by time urgency, impatience, and, often, hostility. Research reveals that it is all right to be in a hurry, but that anger needs to be handled effectively because it is the hostile element of the Type A profile that increases the risk of coronary heart disease.   Pages: 319-321

1. You don't usually think about your phone number, but if someone asked you for it, you could easily recall it and make yourself aware of it. Your phone number is likely stored in your:

Answer: (C) preconscious.   Page: 341

2. George wants a new stereo badly. He decides he will buy a new one by putting it on his credit card, without worrying too much about the debt he is accruing. George is acting based on the wishes of his:

Answer: (A) id.   Page: 341

3. Alice feels good about how neat and organized she keeps her room. This pride comprises her:

Answer: (D) ego ideal.   Pages: 341-342

4. Lysette cannot believe it when her friends tell her that her boy friend is cheating on her. She insists they must be mistaken. Which Freudian defense mechanism might Lysette be exhibiting?

Answer: (D) denial   Page: 342

5. Tabitha has always been a flirtatious and promiscuous woman. She is very vain, and she tends to seek attention from anyone around her. Freud might suggest that she had problems at which psychosexual stage of development?

Answer: (B) phallic   Page: 343

6. Which theorist suggested that we share the universal experiences of humankind throughout evolution?

Answer: (A) Carl Jung   Page: 344

7. Which theorist suggested that behavior, cognitive factors, and the environment have a mutually influential relationship?

Answer: (C) Albert Bandura   Page: 347

8. Which of the following statements about the differences between people with high self-efficacy and low self-efficacy is *false*?

Answer: (B) People with high self-efficacy set lower goals that are more realistic than those with self-efficacy.   Page: 347

9. Someone with an internal locus of control is most likely to explain a high test grade as due to:

Answer: (C) hard work.   Page: 347

10. Which group of theories is most likely to suggest that individuals can reach their full potential for growth?

Answer: (D) humanistic   Page: 348

11. Ben goes along with what his friends want to do even though he would prefer to do something else. He does so because he wants to be accepted. Carl Rogers would explain Ben's behavior as saying that he has been exposed to:

Answer: (A) conditions of worth.   Pages: 348-349

12. You are trying to set up two of your friends for a date. One asks you to describe the other's personality, which you do using 5-8 characteristics. According to Allport, what kind of traits have you listed?

Answer: (C) central traits   Page: 349

13. Zach is an emotional, nervous, and moody person, but he is always good-natured, warm, and cooperative. On which two Big Five traits would Zach likely be rated highly?

Answer: (D) agreeableness and neuroticism   Pages: 350-351

14. According to the Minnesota twin study, which of the following statements concerning twins and personality is *true*?

Answer: (A) Identical twins are similar on several personality factors, whether reared together or apart.   Page: 352

15. Genes exert more influence on which Big Five traits?

Answer: (a) extroversion and neuroticism   Page: 353

16. Nicole responds to some questionnaires that ask her questions about her behaviors and personality characteristics. What kind of personality assessment has she undergone?

Answer: (b) a personality inventory   Page: 355

17.   Which of the following provides a standardized format for the data from observations or interviews?

Answer: (B) a rating scale   Page: 355

18.   Which of the following is often used by career counselors?

Answer: (B) the Myers-Briggs Type Indicator (MBTI)   Page: 358

19.   Which of the following is a projective test?

Answer: (C) the Thematic Apperception Test (TAT)   Page: 359

20.   Which of the following is considered by the examiner in evaluating responses to the Rorschach Inkblot Test?

Answer: (D) all of the above are considered   Page: 358

21.   The ego operates according to a principle that demands immediate gratification.

Answer: False   Page: 341

22.   Freud's theories have been criticized as defying scientific testing.

Answer: True   Page: 344

23.   Low self-efficacy has been related to an increased risk for depression.

Answer: True   Page: 347

24.   People with an internal locus of control are more likely to procrastinate than individuals with an external locus of control.

Answer: False   Page: 347

25.   According to Maslow, self-actualized individuals are autonomous and thus do not pursue personal relationships.

Answer: False   Page: 348

26.   Observable qualities of personality are referred to as source traits.

Answer: False   Pages: 349-350

27.   The Big Five factors have been found in cross-cultural studies in Canada, Poland, Germany, Hong Kong, and Portugal.

Answer: True   Page: 351

28.   The trait of aggressiveness is more influenced by parental upbringing than by genetics.

Answer: False   Pages: 352-353

29.   The MMPI contains validity scales to detect faking or lying.

Answer: True   Page: 357

30.   The Rorschach Inkblot Test continues to have poor interrater agreement due to the lack of a scoring system.

Answer: False   Pages: 358-359

31.   What are the primary distinctions between the theories of the Neo-Freudians and Freud's theory?

Answer: Compared to Freud's psychoanalytic theory, the Neo-Freudians, including Jung, Adler, and Horney, tended to look more at the life span of an individual in shaping personality, rather than suggesting tat personality was completely formed in childhood. They focused more on the unity of the individual self than on intrapsychic conflicts, and they tended to place less emphasis on sexual impulses, and the id in general, than did Freud. Greater emphasis was placed on the development of one's identity. Horney in particular argued against Freud's views of women, including his notion that a woman's desire to have a child and a man is a conversion of her unfulfilled wish for a penis.   Pages: 344-346

32.   Describe the situation vs. trait debate.

Answer: The situation-trait debate is an ongoing discussion among psychologists about the relative importance of factors within the situation and factors within the person in accounting for behavior. Mischel and others argue that individuals behave differently in different situations. Advocates of the trait side of the debate argue that support for trait theories has come from many longitudinal studies. Current evidence supports the view that there are internal traits that strongly influence behavior across situations, but that situational variables do affect personality traits. Pages: 351-352

33.   How does personality differ based on the individualism/collectivism dimension of a culture?

Answer: In individualist cultures, more emphasis is placed on individual achievement than on group achievement. High achieving individuals are accorded honor and prestige. The United States is an individualistic culture. People in collectivist cultures, on the other hand, tend to be more interdependent and define themselves and their personal interests in terms of their group membership. Several Latin American cultures, such as Guatemala and Ecuador, are collectivist cultures. The culture's emphasis is thought to predict which types of behaviors and traits would thus be more valued within that culture. For example, autonomy is thought to be more valued in individualist cultures, whereas respect for harmonious social relationships may be more valued in collectivist cultures. Some psychologists warn against overemphasizing cultural differences in personality, arguing that the goal of all individuals, regardless of cultural context, is to enhance self-esteem.   Pages: 354-355

1.   Which of the following is not an element of one's personality, according to the text definition?

Answer: (D) biological mechanisms   Page: 340

2.   You stare at the clock during class, very aware of how slowly the time seems to pass. This awareness is contained in your:

Answer: (B) conscious.   Page: 341

3.   Kia feels guilty for lying to a friend. This guilt is part of her:

Answer: (B) conscience.   Page: 341

4.   The ego operates according to the reality principle, which means the ego

Answer: (A) considers the constraints of the environment while trying to satisfy id impulses.
          Page: 341

5.   Which is the correct order of Freud's stages?

Answer: (D) oral, anal, phallic, latency, genital   Page: 343

6.   According to Freud, what process leads to superego development?

Answer: (C) identification   Page: 342

7.   Which theorist suggested that inferiority feelings could prevent personal development?

Answer: (D) Alfred Adler   Page: 345

8.   Horney disagreed with Freud on:

Answer: (D) all of the above.   Pages: 345-346

9.   Which group of theories is most likely to suggest that personality is shaped most by childhood experiences?

Answer: (A) psychoanalytic   Page: 340

10.   Which of the following is *not* part of Bandura's concept of reciprocal determinism?

Answer: (C) unconscious conflicts   Page: 347

11.   Someone with an external locus of control is most likely to explain a high test grade as due to:

Answer: (B) an easy exam.   Page: 347

12.   Which is an aspect of Rogers' person-centered therapy that contributes to the development of a fully-functioning person?

Answer: (C) unconditional positive regard   Page: 349

13.   Lee is a careful person. In fact, if you asked him to describe his entire personality in one word, he'd say the word would be "careful." According to Allport, careful is Lee's

Answer: (A) cardinal trait.   Page: 349

14.   Which personality test did Raymond Cattell develop?

Answer: (B) the Sixteen Personality Factors Questionnaire (16PF)   Page: 350

15.   Trait theories:

Answer: (D) look at personal characteristics that are stable across situations.   Page: 349

16.   What do adoption studies say about hereditary influences on personality?

Answer: (B) Adopted children are most similar in personality to their biological parents.
        Page: 353

17.   People in individualistic cultures:

Answer: (C) are accorded honor and prestige for personal achievement.   Page: 354

18.   Which of the following does *not* increase the accuracy of behavioral assessment?

Answer: (A) using projective tests   Page: 355

19.   The Minnesota Multiphasic Personality Inventory (MMPI):

Answer: (D) all of the above   Pages: 355-356

20.   Why are projective tests "projective"?

Answer: (C) The subjects project their unconscious thoughts and feelings onto the test.
        Page: 358

21.   Several studies have shown that people do try to repress unpleasant thoughts.

Answer: True   Page: 342

22.   While Freud's theory was popular a long time ago, no one today believes it offers anything of value to our understanding of personality.

Answer: False   Page: 344

23.   The tendency for people to believe in a god is an archetype.

Answer: True   Page: 345

24.   Self-efficacy is based on objective standards of performance.

Answer: False   Page: 347

25.   Self-esteem is based in part on comparisons of actual to desired traits.

Answer: True   Page: 349

26.   Scores on the Big Five have been related to the characteristics of someone's home.

Answer: True   Page: 351

27.   Consistent with the stereotype of "grumpy old men," agreeableness declines as we age.

Answer: False   Page: 352

28.   Genes serve to constrain the ways in which environments affect personality traits.

Answer: True   Page: 353

29.   The United States is ranked as the most individualistic culture, such that minority groups within the U.S. also become individualistic.

Answer: False   Page: 354

30.   The halo effect happens when an interviewer focuses on positive traits of an interviewee that are irrelevant to the purpose of the interview.

Answer: True   Page: 355

31.   Name and describe five Freudian defense mechanisms.

Answer: Freud proposed that defense mechanisms serve to minimize the anxiety that can arise from internal conflicts and to protect self-esteem. Repression is the involuntary removal of an unpleasant memory, thought, perception, or impulse from consciousness. Denial is refusing to acknowledge that a threat or danger exists. Projection involves attributing one's own undesirable traits, thoughts, behavior, or impulses to another person. Reaction formation involves expressing exaggerated ideas and emotions that are the opposite of disturbing, unconscious impulses and desires. Finally, displacement involves substituting a less threatening object or person for the original object of a sexual or aggressive impulse.   Pages: 342-344

32.   Name and describe the traits that comprise the five-factor theory of personality.

Answer: The Big Five refers to five dimensions that are believed to suffice in explaining personality. A person's personality is described by indicating how he or she rates on each of these five dimensions. Each dimension combines traits that are similar or occur together. For example, someone who is high in extraversion is likely to be described as sociable, outgoing, and active. Someone high in neuroticism is likely to be described as moody, irritable, nervous, and inclined to worry. Someone high in conscientiousness is likely to be described as dependable, reliable, responsible, thorough, and hard-working. Someone high in agreeableness is likely to be described as pleasant, good-natured, warm, sympathetic, and cooperative. Finally, someone high in openness is likely to be described as imaginative, intellectually curious, and broad-minded. Pages: 350-351

33.   Distinguish between projective and objective methods for personality assessment, providing examples of each.

Answer: Personality assessment is used in both clinical and nonclinical settings, and different approaches to it have been designed to serve different purposes. The tests used may be either objective or projective: Objective tests are designed to elicit conscious responses and minimize the influence of subjective elements (opinions, for example) on the results; projective techniques are designed to explore the unconscious. Objective approaches are often in the form of personality inventories that ask the test taker to select a response to a series of statements. The MMPI, for example, requires a response of "true," "false," or "cannot say" to a series of statements about behaviors, thoughts, and feelings. The MMPI is designed to detect abnormality and was constructed using the responses of individuals with psychiatric disorders. Projective tests are often used by psychoanalysts, as they are designed to reveal the unconscious by asking the test taker to project his or her thoughts and feelings onto some ambiguous stimulus. The most well-known projective test is probably the Rorschach Inkblot Method, which requires the test taker to describe what she or he sees in an inkblot. The belief is that the description given will reveal something that the respondent may not want to admit or may not be aware of. Pages: 355-359

1.   Gretchen likes to keep everything. She has things stacked in corners and every closet is filled to the top. Lots of people save things, but Gretchen's "saving" has reached the point that every surface in her home is covered. She is embarrassed to have company – yet she continues to "save" things. What is it about Gretchen's behavior that makes it considered "abnormal?"

Answer: (B) it is maladaptive   Page: 369

2.   Which perspective contends that early childhood experiences are behind the manifestation of psychological disorders?

Answer: (B) psychodynamic   Page: 371

3.   Which type of disorder has the highest lifetime prevalence in the U.S.?

Answer: (C) anxiety disorders   Page: 370

4.   Eric does not like to be in public places – especially where there are a lot of people and getting away would be difficult. He fears he will have a panic attack and not be able to get away or get help. Eric could probably be diagnosed with:

Answer: (A) agoraphobia.   Page: 374

5.   Which of the following would be considered a social phobia?

Answer: (C) fear of public speaking   Page: 375

6.   Mark is a "clean freak." He spends hours upon hours mopping, dusting, and in general sanitizing his house. Mark's cleaning behaviors might be described as:

Answer: (D) a compulsion.   Page: 376

7.   Which patient is most at risk for a recurrent episode of depression?

Answer: (C) Carol, who first became depressed at age 14   Pages: 377-378

8.   The rate of depression among women is generally _____ that of men.

Answer: (B) twice   Page: 377

9.   Which factors play a major role in bipolar and major depressive episodes?

Answer: (A) biological and cognitive   Page: 379

10.   The word "psychotic" refers to:

Answer: (C) loss of contact with reality.   Page: 381

11.   Marianne believes that she is a world-famous movie star. Her neighbors see her occasionally in her front yard, waving to them -- as if they were her adoring crowd. Marianne suffers from:

Answer: (A) delusions of grandeur.   Page: 381

12.   Schizophrenia has been associated with abnormal activity of the neurotransmitter:

Answer: (D) dopamine.   Page: 382

13.   Individuals with which type of schizophrenia have periods where they display little or no body movement, often remaining in bizarre positions for hours?

Answer: (D) catatonic   Page: 383

14.   Which of the following disorders is diagnosed more often in men than women?

Answer: (C) schizophrenia   Page: 384

15.   Following an accident, Michael became blind. Doctors can find no medical cause for his blindness. They should consider a diagnosis of:

Answer: (a) a conversion disorder.   Page: 385

16.   The disorder that involves an individual having several different personalities, one host and at least one alter. This disorder is called:

Answer: (A) dissociative identity disorder.   Page: 386

17.   Sarah is a female but she believes she should be a male. Sarah's problem might be considered an example of:

Answer: (A) a gender identity disorder.   Page: 387

18.   James finds it arousing when his girl friend wears a sexy negligee. James would be diagnosed with:

Answer: (D) no disorder at all.   Page: 369, 387

19.   Which cluster of personality disorders includes disorders that are most likely to be confused with schizophrenia, especially paranoid schizophrenia?

Answer: (A) cluster A   Page: 387

20.   Tina is one of those people you can never predict. One minute she's your best friend; the next, she hates you and considers you to be her worst enemy. She has fits of inappropriate anger, recklessness and occasional suicidal gestures. Tina may be an example of:

Answer: (C) a borderline personality disorder.   Page: 387

21.   Insanity is a term used by mental health professionals to describe those suffering from psychological disorders.

Answer: False   Page: 369

22.   Mental illness is diagnosed in 20 times more Americans than is cancer.

Answer: True   Page: 370

23.   Antidepressant drugs are effectively used in the treatment of obsessive-compulsive disorder (OCD).

Answer: True   Page: 376

24.   Research indicates that one year after their initial diagnosis of major depressive disorder, over 90% of patients still show symptoms.

Answer: False   Page: 377

25.   About 90% of individuals who commit suicide leave clues.

Answer: True   Page: 380

26.   Schizophrenia involves the possession of multiple personalities within the same body.

Answer: False   Page: 381

27.   Smelling something that is not there is an example of a hallucination.

Answer: True   Page: 381

28.   A hypochondriac is someone who fakes an illness to get attention.

Answer: False   Page: 385

29.   Dissociative amnesia may be caused by a traumatic head injury that impairs the functioning of the hippocampus.

Answer: False   Page: 385

30.   Genes strongly influence the development of gender identity disorder.

Answer: True   Page: 387

31.   Review the questions that may be asked to determine whether someone's behavior is abnormal.

Answer: Human behavior lies along a continuum, from well adjusted to maladaptive. Several questions may be asked to determine where along this continuum behavior becomes abnormal. First, is the behavior considered strange within the person's own culture? One reason for this question is to rule out judging someone as abnormal because of a specific cultural custom or behavior. Does the behavior cause personal distress? If a behavior causes an individual considerable emotional distress, the behavior may warrant being considered abnormal. Is the behavior maladaptive? A normal behavior should not lead to impaired functioning. Is the person a danger to self or others? To be committed to a mental hospital a person must be considered mentally ill and endangering themselves or someone else. Is the person legally responsible for their acts? The legal term *insanity* is used to describe someone whose psychiatric state makes them not legally responsible for their actions.   Page: 369

32.   Describe the risk factors for suicide, including gender, age, and ethnic differences in suicide rates.

Answer: Depression is one significant risk factor for suicide, but not all depressed people are suicidal. Other risk factors include other mood disorders, schizophrenia, and substance abuse. Life stressors can also increase suicide risk. In the U.S., White Americans and Native Americans have similar suicide rates, and both groups are more likely to commit suicide than African Americans and Hispanic Americans. Asian Americans have the lowest suicide rate of all ethnic groups in the United States. Women are generally four times more likely than men to attempt suicide, but men are more likely to succeed, as they tend to choose more lethal methods. Finally, older Americans are at a higher risk of suicide than teens and young adults. Risk factors for older adults to commit suicide include poor general health, serious illness, loneliness, and decline in economic status.   Pages: 380-381

33.   Distinguish between positive and negative symptoms of schizophrenia.

Answer: Schizophrenia is a serious and complicated mental illness and each of its symptoms can be classified as either positive or negative. Positive, in this instance, refers to something being present and negative, to something being absent. Positive symptoms are the abnormal behaviors that are seen in those with schizophrenia and might include hallucinations, delusions, and derailment. Negative symptoms would include social withdrawal, a lack of emotion, and limited movement, normal behaviors that are missing.   Pages: 382-382

1.   Velma is deathly afraid of elevators. She works on the fifth floor of an office building, so she climbs the stairs to and from work each day. She makes sure she is never late, and, in general, her avoidance of elevators doesn't cause her any problems, other than her own secret embarrassment over what she considers a "silly fear." By which criterion would Velma's behavior be considered abnormal?

Answer: (B) it is maladaptive   Page: 369

2.   Which perspective is based on the belief that abnormal behavior is caused by problems such as chemical imbalances or genetics?

Answer: (B) biological   Page: 371

3.   Which psychological disorder has the highest annual prevalence rate in the United States?

Answer: (C) specific phobia   Page: 370

4.   Chronic, excessive worry for six months or more is called a(n):

Answer: (A) generalized anxiety disorder   Page: 373

5.   The most common type of specific phobia involves:

Answer: (C) fears of situations like elevators or heights.   Page: 375

6.   Persistent, recurrent, involuntary thoughts or images that invade the consciousness and cause personal distress are called:

Answer: (A) obsessions.   Page: 376

7.   Jerry feels sad and guilty. He says that his life is meaningless and he feels helpless. Based only on this information, you suspect that Jerry is suffering from a mood disorder called:

Answer: (C) major depression.   Page: 377

8.   Abnormal levels of which neurotransmitter are most strongly linked to depression and suicidal thoughts?

Answer: (D) serotonin   Page: 379

9.   Which ethnic group in the U.S. is most likely to commit suicide?

Answer: (B) White Americans   Page: 380

10.   Hallucinations are an example of a:

Answer: (C) positive symptom.   Page: 381

11.   Clay has been diagnosed with schizophrenia. He is difficult to understand when he speaks, because he shifts from one subject to another without any real warning or connection. This symptom is called:

Answer: (A) derailment.   Page: 381

12.   Marcus shows almost no emotional expression. He speaks in a monotone voice and seems more like a robot than a person. Marcus is exhibiting:

Answer: (D) flat affect.   Page: 382

13.   Which of the following is not a brain abnormality found in people with schizophrenia?

Answer: (C) higher levels of neural activity in the frontal lobes   Page: 382

14.   Which of the following statements about gender differences in schizophrenia is *false*?

Answer: (C) Men respond better to treatment of schizophrenia than women.   Page: 384

15.   Aaron is preoccupied with his physical health. If he gets a cold, he is sure it is pneumonia. Every headache leads him to the doctor – convinced he has a brain tumor. Aaron most likely has a disorder called:

Answer: (D) hypochondriasis.   Page: 385

16.   Carrie suffers a complete loss of memory, including personal identity. She travels far away from home and assumes a new identity. Which disorder best fits Carrie?

Answer: (B) dissociative fugue   Page: 386

17.   What percentage of patients with dissociative identity disorder are women?

Answer: (D) 90%   Page: 386

18.   For which type of disorder is someone most likely to be treated with Viagra?

Answer: (A) a sexual dysfunction   Page: 386

19.   Which of the following would *not* be considered a paraphilia?

Answer: (C) the desire to change sexes   Page: 387

20.   Ted Bundy was charming and likeable, at first. But Ted Bundy was a serial killer –
completely devoid of a conscience. He killed with no remorse; he had a complete disregard for
the rights of others. Ted Bundy was considered to have:

Answer: (D) an antisocial personality.   Pages: 387-388

21.   The term "intern syndrome" has been used to describe the tendency for individuals
learning about disorders to notice that they or someone they know have some of the symptoms
described.

Answer: True   Page: 368

22.   To be committed to a mental hospital, the only criterion is whether an individual has a
psychological disorder.

Answer: False   Page: 369

23.   The lifetime prevalence for depression is higher in the United States than any other
country.

Answer: False   Page: 377

24.   Phobias are most often treated using medications such as Valium.

Answer: False   Page: 375

25.   Severely depressed people may suffer from delusions or hallucinations.

Answer: True   Page: 377

26.   Individuals with bipolar disorder typically cycle between depressed and manic states with
no periods of normalcy as long as they go untreated.

Answer: False   Page: 379

27.   Women are more likely than men to attempt suicide, but men are more likely to be
successful in committing suicide.

Answer: True   Page: 380

28.   Cocaine abuse can alter dopamine activity in the brain and increase risk for schizophrenia.

Answer: True   Page: 382

29.   Approximately 95% of patients with dissociative identity disorder report early histories of severe trauma or abuse.

Answer: True   Page: 386

30.   Individuals with a personality disorder tend to respond well to medications, but not therapy.

Answer: False   Page: 387

31.   Review how the biological, biopsychosocial, psychodynamic, learning, and cognitive perspectives each explain psychological disorders.

Answer: Different theoretical perspectives explain what causes, and how to treat, psychological disorders differently. The biological perspective assumes that a psychological disorder is a symptom of an underlying physical disorder caused by a structural or biological abnormality in the brain, by genetic inheritance, or by infection. The biopsychosocial perspective proposes that psychological disorders result from a combination of biological, psychological, and social causes. The psychodynamic perspective posits that psychological disorders stem from early childhood experiences and unresolved, unconscious sexual or aggressive conflicts. The learning perspective states that abnormal thoughts, feelings, and behaviors are learned and sustained like any other behaviors, or that there is a failure to learn appropriate behaviors. Finally, the cognitive perspective asserts that faulty thinking or distorted perceptions can cause psychological disorders.   Pages: 371-372

32.   Review the subtypes of schizophrenia.

Answer: Certain features distinguish different subtypes of schizophrenia. Paranoid schizophrenia usually includes delusions of grandeur or persecution. People with this subtype often show exaggerated anger or suspiciousness. Disorganized schizophrenia is the most serious type, marked by extreme social withdrawal, hallucinations, delusions, silliness, inappropriate laughter, grimaces, and other bizarre behavior. People with this disorder often show flat or inappropriate affect, and are often incoherent. Their behavior is inappropriate, and they have the poorest chance of recovery. Catatonic schizophrenia involves movement disturbances, often in the form of stillness or stupor, or excitement and agitation. People with this disorder may become frozen in a position for hours at a time without moving. Finally, the term undifferentiated schizophrenia is used when the schizophrenic symptoms do not neatly fit any of the other specific types of schizophrenia.   Pages: 382-383

33.   Describe the behaviors that are associated with the three clusters of personality disorders.

Answer: Personality disorders are long-standing, inflexible, maladaptive patterns of behaving and relating to others, which usually begins in early childhood or adolescence. *DSM-IV-TR* divides the personality disorders into clusters, and the disorders within each cluster share certain similarities. Cluster A disorders are characterized by odd behavior. Individuals with paranoid personality disorder are extremely suspicious, and those with schizoid personality disorder isolate themselves from others. People with schizotypal personality disorder demonstrate odd thought patterns and a lack of social skills. Cluster B disorders are characterized by erratic, overly dramatic behavior. Individuals with these disorders are at a higher risk for self-harm than other personality disorders. Cluster C disorders are characterized by intense feelings of anxiety, either associated with a disruption of routines (as in obsessive-compulsive personality disorder) or with social relationships (as in avoidant or dependent personality disorders).   Pages: 387-388

1.   Which group of therapy approaches are based on the notion that psychological well-being depends on self-understanding?

Answer: (C) insight therapies   Page: 397

2.   Which approach attempts to uncover childhood experiences in order to explain current difficulties?

Answer: (A) psychodynamic therapy   Page: 398

3.   Valora became angry with her therapist and shouted at him, "You are just like my father!" Freud would consider this an example of:

Answer: (C) transference.   Page: 398

4.   What is the goal of person-centered therapy?

Answer: (B) to assist the client's growth toward self-actualization   Page: 399

5.   The individual most associated with Gestalt therapy is:

Answer: (A) Fritz Perls.   Page:399

6.   Interpersonal therapy (IPT) is especially helpful in treating:

Answer: (D) depression.   Page: 400

7.   Which type of problem is Interpersonal therapy (IPT) *not* specifically designed to address?

Answer: (C) behavioral problems exhibited in school   Page: 400

8.   One factor that is associated with relapse rates among schizophrenic patients is family members with:

Answer: (B) high EE.   Page: 400

9.   Juan's school uses a reward system for doing homework and good behavior. Children earn gold stars for completing assignments and paying attention to the teacher, and later can exchange stars for snacks or even a day without homework. Which behavior modification technique is Juan's school using?

Answer: (D) token economy   Page: 402

10.   Which technique is designed to treat phobias by exposing the client to extended periods of contact with the feared object or event until the anxiety decreases?

Answer: (B) flooding   Page: 404

11.   Exposure and response prevention is an approach that has been successful treating:

Answer: (D) obsessive-compulsive disorder. Page: 404

12.   In Ellis' ABCs, the A represents:

Answer: (D) the activating event.   Page: 406

13.   Joan's therapist encourages her to put her beliefs to the test in real-world "tests." Which approach is her therapist taking?

Answer: (A) cognitive therapy   Page: 407

14.   Neuroleptics is another term for:

Answer: (A) antipsychotics.   Page:408

15.   Which drug is someone most likely to take for bipolar disorder?

Answer: (C) lithium   Page: 409

16.   Cynthia wants to be a psychiatrist. What degree will she need after college?

Answer: (B) M.D.   Page: 413

17.   The bond between therapist and client that is thought to be a factor in the effectiveness of psychotherapy is called:

Answer: (D) therapeutic alliance.   Page: 414

18.   What does the research suggest about the success of psychotherapy?

Answer: (B) The longer someone is in therapy, the more improvement they seem to make.
        Page: 413

19.   Which of the following behaviors would be considered unethical for a therapist?

Answer: (C) treating an ex-girl friend in therapy   Page: 414

20.   Culturally sensitive therapy is important because:

Answer: (B) cultural factors need o be considered when choosing a therapeutic intervention.
        Page: 414

21.   A psychodynamic therapist would interpret a client's being late to a session as a form of resistance.

Answer: True   Page: 398

22.   Person-centered therapy is an example of a directive therapy.

Answer: False   Page: 399

23.   A gestalt therapist might help a client with unfinished business using the empty chair technique.

Answer: True   Page: 399

24.   Family therapy tends to be ineffective as a treatment option for adolescent drug abuse.

Answer: False   Page: 400

25.   Alcoholics Anonymous (AA) is a form of self-help group.

Answer: True   Page: 401

26.   Aversion therapy is no longer utilized due to ethical concerns.

Answer: False   Page: 404

27.   Tardive dyskinesia is a movement disorder brought on by long-term use of antidepressants.

Answer: False   Page: 408

28.   Maintenance doses of antidepressants may be needed following a major depressive episode to reduce the probability of a relapse.

Answer: True   Page: 409

29.   Rapid transcranial magnetic stimulation (rTMS) appears to have the benefits of electroconvulsive therapy (ECT) with significantly fewer risks.

Answer: True   Page: 411

30.   Therapists can actually be too sensitive to gender issues and assume an incorrect cause for problems as a result.

Answer: True   Page: 416

31.   Compare and contrast Ellis' rational emotive therapy and Beck's cognitive therapy.

Answer: Both Ellis' rational emotive therapy and Beck's cognitive therapy are forms of cognitive therapies, which assume that maladaptive behavior can result from irrational thoughts, beliefs, and ideas, which the therapist tries to change. Ellis' rational emotive therapy approach relies on his ABC theory, in which the activating event (A) does not cause emotions, but the person's belief (B) about the event that causes emotional consequences (C). Ellis's approach does not involve a warm, supportive therapist, but one who challenges the client's irrational thinking that leads to emotional distress. Beck's cognitive therapy traces emotional distress to an individual's automatic thoughts, unreasonable but unquestioned ideas that rule the person's life. Beck's approach is designed to help clients stop their negative thoughts and replace them with more objective thoughts. Beck's approach accomplishes this goal through guidance of the client so that personal experiences can provide evidence in the real world to refute the false beliefs. Both approaches have similar goals, but accomplish them through differing strategies.
Pages: 406-407

32.   What are the three types of drugs used to treat depression, and how do they work?

Answer: The antidepressants are the tricyclics, the selective serotonin reuptake inhibitors (SSRIs), and the monoamine oxidase (MAO) inhibitors. The tricyclic antidepressants act to block the reuptake of norepinephrine and serotonin, treating the depression by increasing the activity of these neurotransmitters. Drugs like Prozac are SSRIs and also work by blocking neurotransmitter reuptake, but block reuptake selectively of serotonin. While the tricyclics and the SSRIs increase neurotransmitter activity by blocking reuptake, the MAO inhibitors do so by blocking the activity of the enzyme that breaks down norepinephrine and serotonin. Thus, all the drugs used to treat depression are drugs that increase the availability of serotonin only (the SSRIs) or of serotonin and norepinephrine. The effectiveness of these drugs suggests that a decrease in the activity of these neurotransmitters is what underlies depression.   Page: 409

33.   Describe five types of mental health professionals, including their training and services provided. Which of them suits your interests?

Answer: Psychiatrists receive a medical degree and undergo a residency in psychiatry. They provide psychotherapy, drug therapy, and hospitalize patients with serious psychological disorders. Clinical psychologists receive a Ph.D. or Psy.D., and complete an internship in clinical psychology. In some states, with additional training, they can also provide drug therapy. School psychologists receive a Ph.D., Ed.D., or master's degree, and complete an internship in school psychology. They primarily assess and treat school problems in children and adolescents, as well as conducting psychological tests. Clinical or psychiatric social workers receive a master's degree and complete an internship in psychiatric social work. They engage in diagnosis and treatment of psychological disorders, and identify supportive community services. Licensed marriage and family therapists receive a master's degree and complete an internship in marriage and family therapy. They conduct assessments and provide therapy for relationship problems.
Pages: 413

Chapter 13 - Practice Test 2

1.   Which group of therapies assumes that people have the freedom and ability to make their own decisions and lead rational lives?

Answer: (B) humanistic   Page: 399

2.   Frank's therapist asks him to say whatever comes to mind. His therapist is employing:

Answer: (A) free association.   Page: 398

3.   The individual most associated with person-centered therapy is:

Answer: (C) Carl Rogers.   Page: 399

4.   Lorraine's therapist encourages her to resolve her issues with her father by speaking to an empty chair as if he were sitting there. The therapist then has Lorraine occupy the chair and respond as her father would. Lorraine is attending:

Answer: (C) gestalt therapy.   Page: 399

5.   For which of the following has family or couples therapy *not* been shown to be effective?

Answer: (D) phobias   Page: 400

6.   Which of the following is *not* a benefit of group therapy?

Answer: (A) Group therapy works more quickly than individual therapy.   Page: 401

7.   A study by Morgan and Flora (2002) demonstrated that those prisoners who participated in group therapy progressed better than those who did not participate for each of the following problems *except*:

Answer: (B) alcoholism.   Page: 401

8.   Which term refers to the systematic application of learning principles to help a person eliminate undesirable behaviors and replace them with adaptive ones?

Answer: (B) behavior modification   Page: 402

9.   Loretta has a fear of spiders. Her therapist trains her to relax, and helps her make a list of situations involving spider that escalate in how much anxiety they provoke. What technique is Loretta's therapist using?

       (C) systematic desensitization   Page: 403

10. Which of the following, used to rid a client of an undesirable habit or harmful behavior such as smoking or drinking, often involves unpleasant associations with electric shock or drugs that induce nausea and vomiting?

Answer: (A) aversion therapy   Page: 404

11. According to Ellis:

Answer: (B) one's beliefs determine how one reacts to an event.   Page: 406

12. Which of the following approaches would be considered a nondirective therapy?

Answer: (D) person centered therapy   Page: 399

13. Jessica puts a lot of pressure on herself in school. She believes that she must make an A on every exam or it means she is stupid. What would Beck call this unreasonable but unquestioned idea that rules Jessica's life?

Answer: (C) an automatic thought   Page: 407

14. For which of the following disorders has cognitive therapy been shown to be effective?

Answer: (D) all of the above   Page: 407

15. Fluoxetine (Prozac) is which kind of drug?

Answer: (B) a selective serotonin reuptake inhibitor (SSRI)   Page: 409

16. What does your text suggest about the effectiveness of medications such as Xanax and Prozac?

Answer: (C) Psychotherapy alone seems to work as well as psychotherapy and drugs together.
          Page: 413

17. Which of the following professionals do *not* conduct psychological tests?

Answer: (A) psychiatrists   Page: 413

18. Which of the following professionals does *not* require a doctoral-level degree?

Answer: (D) licensed professional counselors   Page: 413

19.   Which of the following is *not* an ethical requirement of professionals doing psychological testing?

Answer: (A) The tests should be completed in a single session so as not to inconvenience the client.   Page: 414

20.   When working with immigrants, which of these do researchers consider to be most important to successful treatment?

Answer: (B) The therapist must be able to separate psychopathology from anxiety and sadness over the immigration experience.   Page: 415

21.   Because psychodynamic therapies require such a commitment of time and expense, they are not utilized at all today except in rare circumstances.

Answer: False   Page: 398

22.   Gestalt therapy helps people become more self-accepting by realizing that their behavior is due to societal influences.

Answer: False   Page: 399

23.   Relationship therapies work with an individual's internal struggles as well as their interpersonal relationships.

Answer: True   Page: 400

24.   When accompanied by medication, family therapy can reduce relapse rates of individuals with schizophrenia.

Answer: True   Page: 400

25.   Time out has been shown to be effective in reducing undesirable behaviors in children and adolescents.

Answer: True   Page: 402

26.   Participant modeling, which is based on observational learning, has been effective in treating depression, but not phobias.

Answer: False   Page: 405

27.   Rational emotive therapy and cognitive therapy have similar goals; they just involve different methods of accomplishing them.

Answer: True   Pages: 406-407

28.   The mental hospital population has increased in number due to the recent breakthroughs in drug therapy.

Answer: False   Page: 408

29.   Selective serotonin reuptake inhibitors (SSRIs) cause irreversible sexual dysfunction.

Answer: False   Page: 409

30.   Gender-sensitive therapy takes into account the effects of gender on both the client *and* the therapist's behavior.

Answer: True   Page: 416

31.   Describe how interpersonal therapy (IPT) addresses interpersonal problems associated with major depression.

Answer: Interpersonal therapy (IPT) is a form of psychotherapy that can be effective in the treatment of depression. This relationship therapy focuses on dealing with four types of problems most commonly associated with major depression, including an extreme response to the loss of a loved one and problems handling interpersonal role disputes. Also addressed may be problems handling transitions and the need to develop interpersonal skills. Regardless of the problem, the approach is to deal with the emotions involved and to seek solutions, either by reevaluating the problem or by taking steps toward an effective resolution.   Page: 400

32.   Describe the use of electroconvulsive therapy (ECT), including the arguments for and against its use.

Answer: Electroconvulsive therapy (ECT) is a biological therapy in which an electric current is passed through the right hemisphere of the brain. It is usually reserved for severely depressed patients who are suicidal. ECT appears to change the biochemical balance in the brain. Some psychiatrists and neurologists have spoken out against ECT, claiming that it causes pervasive brain damage and memory loss. Studies have not revealed structural brain damage from ECT. Pages: 410-411

33. Review the research on the effectiveness of psychotherapy.

Answer: Classic studies of therapy effectiveness have found that any therapy is more effective than no treatment at all, with little difference in effectiveness when comparing therapy approaches directly. A study conducted in *Consumer Reports* indicated that generally, patients believed they benefited substantially from therapy, and were generally satisfied, regardless of whether it was provided by a psychiatrist, psychologist, or social worker. Generally, the longer someone stayed in therapy, the more they improved, and therapy appears to work as well with or without the inclusion of drug therapy. It appears that individual comfort with a therapist and therapy style are more important for effectiveness than simply suggesting that any one approach is superior to the others.   Pages: 411-413

1.   In Stanley Milgram's obedience study, the "learner" was actually a:

Answer: (A) confederate.   Page: 425

2.   Your Grandma always told you that first impressions create lasting impressions. She is essentially describing:

Answer: (C) the primacy effect.   Page: 426

3.   Creighton's boss is particularly grumpy today. He knows that she's been under a lot of stress at home, and figures that is the reason for her grumpiness. Creighton is making:

Answer: (D) a situational attribution.   Page: 427

4.   Shea failed her law school entrance exams. She said it was because there was too much noise in the room and the questions were ridiculous. Shea's excuses are an example of:

Answer: (D) self-serving bias.   Page: 427

5.   Heather never gave Bobby much thought until she found out that he likes her. Lately she's been thinking that she likes him, too. Her attraction is largely based on:

Answer: (A) the mere exposure effect.   Page: 428

6.   Which of the following is a major factor in attractiveness?

Answer: (D) symmetry   Page: 428

7.   The matching hypothesis is similar to the idea that:

Answer: (A) birds of a feather flock together.   Page: 429

8.   Changing or adopting an attitude or behavior to be consistent with social norms of a group or their expectation is called:

Answer: (B) conformity.   Page: 430

9.   Which of the following is a similarity in Milgram and Asch's results?

Answer: (C) In both studies, if at least one other person refused to conform or obey, the participant was less likely to conform or obey as well.   Pages: 425, 431

10.   Phillip was offered a job with weekends off. Once he said yes and gave notice at his old job, the new employer told him he would have to work every Saturday until noon. Phillip's new boss used the:

Answer: (D) low ball technique.   Page:432

11.   Two teams were playing a game of tug-of-war. Gerald was tired, so he just pretended to be pulling – knowing that no one could tell the difference. Gerald's approach to the game is an example of:

Answer: (C) social loafing.   Page: 433

12.   If you work better in front of other people, the effect of those other people is called:

Answer: (A) an audience effect in social facilitation.   Page:

13.   Investigations following the latest NASA shuttle disaster suggested that many of the engineers and others saw problems but failed to speak up because no one else did. They all work well together and were accustomed to everything working properly. In their zeal to launch the shuttle and continue to work effectively and cohesively, they failed to investigate problems that were quite evident. Some suggested that the NASA scientists were victims of:

Answer: (A) groupthink.   Page: 431

14.   Zimbardo's prison study showed that:

Answer: (A) social roles influence behavior.   Page: 434

15.   Which of the following is a deliberate attempt to change the attitude or behavior of another person?

Answer: (B) persuasion   Page: 437

16.   Frank is overweight and seems unable to stick to any diet. Although his diet efforts suggest that he wants to lose weight, he denies it and says that he is happy with his body the way it is. Frank is trying to reduce his feelings of:

Answer: (A) cognitive dissonance.   Page: 436

17.   Which of the following is *not* one of the identified elements of persuasion?

Answer: (C) the decision-making process   Page: 438

18.   When Kitty Genovese was stabbed to death near her apartment, later investigations found that nearly forty people witnessed the attack – yet none called for help for the woman. Some would say that this is an example of:

Answer: (C) the bystander effect.   Page: 439

19.   What did Cloninger find with regard to crime, aggression and biology?

Answer: (B) Adopted children are more likely to be criminals if adoptive parents are criminals.
        Page: 440

20.   Kathy's sorority has a rule against dating boys from certain fraternities. Kathy may only date boys who belong to two specific fraternities. Her sorority considers any other boys to be "undesirables." According to the definitions in your chapter, Kathy's sorority is an example of a(n):

Answer: (A) in-group.   Page: 445

21.   Research has indicated that Americans are more likely to make situational attributions than Koreans for both desirable and undesirable behaviors.

Answer: False   Page: 427

22.   There are significant cultural differences in attractiveness ratings of the opposite sex.

Answer: False   Page: 428

23.   According to Asch's conformity experiments, 75% of the participants conformed to the incorrect response of the majority at least once.

Answer: True   Page: 431

24.   Research indicates that in the presence of others, people's performance suffers on easier tasks but excels on more difficult tasks.

Answer: False   Page: 433

25.   Social loafing is more common in collectivistic cultures like China than here in the United States.

Answer: False   Page: 434

26.   Zimbardo's Stanford prison experiment had to be ended in six days because the behavior of the participants began to get out of hand.

Answer: True   Page: 434

27.   Generally speaking, people with low IQs are easier to persuade than people with high IQs.

Answer: True   Page: 437

28.   Being altruistic carries no benefits for the altruistic person.

Answer: False   Page: 438

29.   Most abusive parents were abused as children.

Answer: False   Page: 444

30.   People perceive more diversity among members of their own ethnic group, and more similarity among members of other groups.

Answer: True   Page: 446

31.   What do men and women rate as the most important qualities in a mate? Review both the similarities and differences in what men and women seek.

Answer: Men and women both consider the physical attractiveness of a partner as a primary consideration in mate selection. Another factor that is important according to research are someone who is similar in personality, physical traits, intellectual ability, education, religion, ethnicity, socioeconomic status, and attitudes. Generally, men and women across a variety of cultures rate four qualities as most important in mate selection: mutual attraction/love, dependable character, emotional stability ad maturity, and a pleasing disposition. According to evolutionary psychologists, men prefer young and beautiful women, because they suggest health of fertility, whereas women prefer someone offering resources and social status. Both sets of qualities are considered adaptive for the next generation.   Page: 429

32.   Describe Stanley Milgram's obedience study. What conclusions could be drawn from it? Could that same study be conducted today?

Answer: Stanley Milgram conducted a study of obedience utilizing male volunteers, in which the student was assigned to be a "teacher" and deliver electric shocks to a "learner" when the learner made errors on a memory task. The teacher was instructed to administer escalating levels of shock with each error by the learner, who was in actuality a confederate of the experimenter. Whenever the teacher hesitated, the experimenter instructed him to continue. At the 20th switch, 300 volts, the learner cried out in pain and pleaded to be let out of the experiment. After the next shock, the learner ceased to respond, and the teacher was instructed to continue. Out of the 40 participants, 26 (or 65%) continued administering shocks to the maximum level, and none stopped before the 20th switch, when the learned cried out and protested. This results of this study suggested that people will follow the orders of an authority figure even if harm may potentially come to another. This study is not as likely to be conducted in that form today, because of concerns about the harm to the teacher participants, even if they are afterward told that the learner is a confederate and was never being shocked at all.   Page: 425, 431-432

33.   Describe the social learning theory of aggression. What does the research evidence say about a relationship between TV violence and viewer aggression?

Answer: The social learning theory of aggression suggests that people learn to behave aggressively by observing aggressive models and by having their aggressive responses reinforced. Aggression is known to be higher in groups and subcultures that condone violent behavior. Albert Bandura's classic "Bobo doll" studies, in which children observed a model playing aggressively with an inflated clown doll were more likely to copy those aggressive behaviors than other children who did not see the aggressive model, demonstrated the potential for aggressive behavior being acquired through observational learning. Research evidence strongly supports a relationship between TV violence and viewer aggression. This relationship is even stronger among individuals who are already highly aggressive. TV violence may stimulate physiological arousal, lower inhibitions, cause unpleasant feelings, and decrease sensitivity to violence and make it more acceptable.   Pages: 443-444

1.   Naomi blames her own poor performance on an exam on her instructor's poor teaching skills. In the next moment, she makes fun of another student who did poorly on the test, saying she knows he is not very smart. Naomi is exhibiting:

Answer: (C) the actor-observer effect.   Page: 427

2.   Beverly's husband is always leaving her little love notes and giving her gifts for no reason at all. She believes his behaviors are because he's a sweet guy. She is making:

Answer: (C) a dispositional attribution.   Page: 427

3.   Which two factors are most likely to contribute to why a man might be attracted to the "girl next door"?

Answer: (A) proximity and mere exposure   Page: 428

4.   Which of the following is most likely to be correct based on social psychology research on attraction?

Answer: (D)   birds of a feather flock together   Page: 429

5.   Mere-exposure effect is contrary to the idea that:

Answer: (A) familiarity breeds contempt.   Page: 428

6.   You are a participant in a conformity study with Solomon Asch. You are most likely to avoid conforming to an incorrect response given by the rest of the group if:

Answer: (B) at least one of the other participants breaks conformity.   Page: 431

7.   In Milgram's original study of obedience, what percentage of participants administered the "maximum" voltage?

Answer: (C) 60%   Page: 431

8.   A technique used to gain a favorable response from someone by first asking small favors is:

Answer: (C) foot-in-the-door technique.   Page: 432

9.   Which of the following is a good way to avoid the effects of social loafing on a group project for class?

Answer: (D) Have the members of the group get individual grades, each based on their own contribution.   Page: 433

10.   Zimbardo's prison experiment was directed at studying:

Answer: (C) social roles.   Page: 434

11.   A supporter of a politician tries to persuade you to vote for his candidate by trying to appeal to fears of what might happen if the opposing candidate wins. This supporter is *most* demonstrating which component of their attitude?

Answer: (A) the emotional component   Page: 435

12.   The more people must sacrifice or suffer in order to become a member of an organization, the more _____ they are likely to become toward the group.

Answer: (A) positive   Page: 436

13.   Under which conditions does an attempt at persuasion work best if it presents both sides of an issue as opposed to just one?

Answer: (D) when the audience is somewhat intelligent   Page: 437

14.   A celebrity is a spokesperson for a product. He is attractive and likeable, and he plays a humorous, if somewhat dumb, character on television. Sales of the product actually decrease once his commercial airs. Why might this be so?

Answer: (C) Persuasion also depends on credibility.   Page: 437

15.   Mr. Arnold donated 5 million dollars to the college for a new student center. He accepted the college's invitation to name the building after him. Mr. Arnold's behavior demonstrates:

Answer: (B) prosocial behavior.   Page: 438

16.   The bystander effect is greatly reduced by:

Answer: (D) public appeal.   Page: 439

17.   Which of the following suggests that aggression results when we make attributions about the motives of people involved when an aversive event occurs?

Answer: (D) the cognitive neoassociationistic model   Page: 442

18.   The general tendency to look at people and situations from the perspective of one's own racial or cultural group is called:

Answer: (C) ethnocentrism.   Page: 446

19.   David is failing algebra. He told his parents not to worry, though. He had decided to ask the Vietnamese student in his class to tutor him, in exchange for his help with English. "Those Asians are always good at math," he said. David's statements are demonstrating a(n):

Answer: (A) stereotype.   Pages: 445-446

20.   Which of the following statements is true, according to your text?

Answer: (B) Most people agree that conditions for minorities are better than 50 years ago.
          Page: 446

21.   Deception is no longer used in social psychology research.

Answer: False   Page:426

22.   Job interviewers are more likely to recommend physically attractive people in part because of the halo effect.

Answer: True   Page: 428

23.   Infants show preferences for attractive faces over unattractive faces.

Answer: True   Page: 428

24.   Research indicates that women are more likely to conform than men.

Answer: False   Page: 431

25.   The presence of others affects our performance due to heightened arousal.

   ·r: True   Page: 433

26. Attitudes predict behavior the majority of the time.

Answer: False   Page: 436

27. Diffusion of responsibility is even more likely to occur during catastrophes because so many more people are involved.

Answer: False   Page: 439

28. The size of personal space varies across individuals and situations.

Answer: True   Page: 443

29. Playing violent video games is correlated with aggression.

Answer: True   Page: 444

30. People often say that they don't engage in more social contact with others of different races due to fear of rejection.

Answer: True   Page: 446

31. Describe the Stanford Prison Experiment by Philip Zimbardo. What conclusion could be drawn from the study?

Answer: The Stanford Prison Experiment was conducted by Philip Zimbardo in the early 1970s to demonstrate the power of social roles in shaping behavior. Social roles are socially defined behaviors that are considered appropriate for individuals occupying certain positions within a given group. In Zimbardo's study, college student volunteers were randomly assigned to be either rguards or prisoners. The guards enforced harsh rules, and the prisoners were stripped naked, searched and deloused. Both groups adapted quickly to their new roles, regardless of preexisting personality characteristics. The experiment, scheduled to last two weeks, was ended after six days. This study demonstrated that social roles can shape behavior quickly and dramatically.   Page: 434

32.   How can cognitive dissonance be applied to a person's smoking behavior?

Answer: Cognitive dissonance is the unpleasant state that can occur when people become aware of inconsistencies between their attitudes, or between their attitudes and their behavior. There are three methods an individual can reduce cognitive dissonance: explaining away the inconsistency, reducing the importance of the inconsistency, or changing behavior. For smokers, the overwhelming evidence linking smoking to a variety of health concerns may lead to dissonance between the desire to be healthy and the unhealthy behavior of smoking. Smokers may choose to explain away the inconsistency, by claiming that they don't really smoke much, or claiming that they will quit before health problems result. They may instead reduce the importance of the inconsistency, by suggesting that their family health history will protect them, or that their other healthy habits will cancel out the negative effects of smoking. Finally, they could instead change the behavior, and quit smoking.   Pages: 436-437

33.   Review the possible biological causes of aggression.

Answer: Aggression is the intentional infliction of physical or psychological harm on others. Personality measures of aggression reveal a heritability estimate of about .50 for aggression, suggestive a strong genetic, and thus a strong biological, component to aggression. One biological factor that has been studied is the low arousal level of the autonomic nervous system (low heart rate and low reactivity), which has been linked to violent behavior. Hormones, specifically high testosterone levels, have been implicated in explaining the higher levels of physical aggression traditionally displayed by men then by women. Brain damage, brain tumors, and temporal love epilepsy have also all been related to aggressive and violent behavior. Finally, alcohol use has been strongly related to aggression, as alcohol and other drugs affect the brain's frontal lobes and disrupt normal executive functions.   Pages: 440, 442

NOTES

NOTES

NOTES

NOTES